MW00987596

In my experience v
about one out of ten
any given time. That's why Jason Lowe's book, *The Church During the Search*, is so needed. Pastors need special kinds of assistance during transition, and so do Pastor Search Committees, but this book ministers uniquely to the entire congregation, especially during the early days when they first find themselves in this position. Those who read it faithfully will find themselves both comforted with biblical compassion and drawn to faith and expectation for the next season of their church's life.

Nate Adams
Executive Director, Illinois Baptist State Association

This book is a unique resource that speaks to the average person in the pew rather than to the Pastor Search Committee. What a needed resource! Having observed Lowe in his varied ministry roles for several years now, I can assure you that he writes as one who is investing his life in seeing the church healthy and flourishing. This resource is an invaluable and lasting contribution to that end.

Paul Chitwood
President, International Mission Board

Occasionally a resource comes about that has the ability to help our churches in a transformational way. Usually these resources break ground in areas that have not been considered before. This is one of those resources. Structuring a book about the Pastor Search Process from the perspective and concerns of the congregant is genius! This insight makes this book a must-have for any church as they navigate the process of finding a new shepherd.

Rick Curtis
Convention and Associational Relations, North American Mission Board

As I previewed this book, I was serving in an intentional interim position. One of my primary roles is helping the church as they transition to a new senior pastor. This book is exactly what the church needed. It is so helpful.

Ron Edmondson
Church Consultant, Pastor, Author

Most churches will experience a senior pastor transition in the next five years, and while there are many resources and consultants to help guide a church's transition team through the pastor search process, Jason provides a resource to church members who are often watching that process from the outside. Even without a senior leader, the mission of the church must and should go on, and the church's members can ensure that it does thanks to Jason helping them consider how to pray, discern, and support their church during this time. This is a much needed, Biblically-based resource that will be a tremendous asset to the Body of Christ.

Josh Ellis
Executive Director, Union Baptist Association

I am pleased to endorse *The Church During the Search: Honoring Christ While You Wait for Your Next Pastor*. This book and study by Jason Lowe will be a consolation and source of encouragement to many churches. I believe God will use this book to bring churches comfort, hope, and continuity of ministry during the difficult time of being without a pastor. I highly recommend it!

Ray Gentry
President and CEO, Southern Baptist Conference of Associational Leaders

Jason Lowe has produced a helpful and much needed resource in *The Church During the Search*. One of the most critical times in the life of a congregation is the time when the church is searching for their next senior pastor. Jason's book, written from the perspective of one who has trained numerous Search Committees, assists churches by providing practical tips. The book is broken down into bite-size segments – thirty daily readings – addressing the most relevant issues related to calling a pastor. Jason's book brings the unbeatable combination of solid research, personal observation, applicable anecdotes, and love for the local church. I highly recommend it.

Todd Gray
Executive Director-Treasurer, Kentucky Baptist Convention

A pastor's departure from a church can be a traumatic event – but it doesn't have to be. Instead, a church can prayerfully and patiently support the search process, trusting God to bring the right next pastor according to His time schedule. In this work, Jason Lowe helps church members consider their own role in the process, and he challenges them to continue being the church in the interim period. The Bible is his guide, and healthy church transitions are his goal. You will find this work helpful, encouraging, and relevant.

Chuck Lawless
Dean of Doctoral Studies and Vice-President of Spiritual Formation and Ministry, Southeastern Baptist Theological Seminary

With *The Church During the Search*, Jason Lowe has given much needed clarity and direction to churches that have just experienced the loss of their pastor. Too often, churches wade through the waters of uncertainty with no plan, direction, or focus – at a time when a Christ-centered plan, biblically based direction, and a spiritual focus are what are needed most. This outstanding resource helps provide this great need.

Sean McMahon
Executive Director, Florida Baptist Association

In my role, I have discovered that the most important decision a church will make is choosing the right pastor. Churches simply do not experience significant spiritual success if the wrong leader is selected. The Pastoral Search Committee (Team) *must* find God's chosen leader! There are helps available for Search Committee members, but little has been written for the average person in the pew. This book is long overdue! Jason brings the practical, helpful perspective of a pastor and Associational Mission Strategist to this work to help church members have a specific plan of involvement during the search process. I know we will use this book as we work with churches, and I'm confident that many others will as well.

Steve Rice
Church Consulting and Revitalization Team Leader, Kentucky Baptist Convention

Jason Lowe has addressed a pressing need. As an Associational Mission Strategist, I spend time training Search Committees how to assist the church in understanding their work, the search process, and the need for prayer and patience. In fact, it is common for me to be asked to come a second time and help the Search Team deal with pressures created by the average church member's misunderstanding of their work. Now I have a resource to share and not just words of advice or anecdotal stories. In *The Church During the Search*, Jason has touched on the most essential topics on which the average church member needs clarification. Jason's knowledge of and love for local churches of all sizes has made this a practical and essential tool for me to have in my toolbelt as I minister to churches in times of ministerial transition. I recommend it to you without reservation.

David Stokes
Lead Mission Strategist, Central Kentucky Network of Baptists

Pastoral transition is hard. The remaining church leadership works for organizational and ministerial continuity. The Pastor Search Committee labors prayerfully to find God's man in God's time. The interim pastor facilitates a positive forward narrative while building the runway for the next pastor. But what is the average church member to do? Surely the faithful church member has an active part to play during the pastoral transition. *The Church During the Search*, by my friend Jason Lowe, will guide church members through seasons of pastoral transition with an active anticipation. I encourage you to work through these pages steadily and prayerfully, learning how your role during this transition is indispensable to the current and future Great Commission success of your church and your next pastor.

Tony Wolfe
Director of Pastor/Church Relations, Southern Baptists of Texas Convention

THE CHURCH
DURING
THE SEARCH

Register This New Book

Benefits of Registering*

- ✓ FREE **replacements** of lost or damaged books
- ✓ FREE **audiobook** – *Pilgrim's Progress*, audiobook edition
- ✓ FREE information about new titles and other **freebies**

www.anekopress.com/new-book-registration

*See our website for requirements and limitations.

THE CHURCH
DURING
THE SEARCH

Honoring Christ While You Wait for Your Next Pastor

JASON LOWE

We love hearing from our readers. Please contact us at www.anekopress.com/questions-comments with any questions, comments, or suggestions.

www.jasonalowe.com

The Church During the Search

© 2020 by Jason Lowe

All rights reserved. Published 2020.

Cover Design: Jonathan Lewis

Editor: Paul Miller

Printed in the United States of America

Aneko Press

www.anekopress.com

Aneko Press, Life Sentence Publishing, and our logos are trademarks of

Life Sentence Publishing, Inc.

203 E. Birch Street

P.O. Box 652

Abbotsford, WI 54405

RELIGION / Christian Church / General

Paperback ISBN: 978-1-62245-709-0

eBook ISBN: 978-1-62245-710-6

10   9   8   7   6   5   4   3   2

Available where books are sold

Contents

Acknowledgments..xi

Introduction xv

Week 1 – Be Prepared...1
   Day 1 – What Just Happened? 3
   Day 2 – Who's Preaching Sunday? 7
   Day 3 – When There Is No News 11
   Day 4 – When Things Don't Go as Planned 17
   Day 5 – The Elephant in the Room 21

Week 2 – Be Informed 27
   Day 1 – Shepherds Feed the Flock 29
   Day 2 – Shepherds Lead the Flock 33
   Day 3 – Shepherds Protect the Flock 37
   Day 4 – Shepherds Comfort the Flock............................41
   Day 5 – Shepherds Must Be Qualified 45

Week 3 – Be Humble..49
   Day 1 – What Your Next Pastor Is Looking for
           in You 51
   Day 2 – Unrealistic Expectations 55
   Day 3 – Disarm the Land Mines......................................61
   Day 4 – When the Past Is the Hero 67
   Day 5 – Deny Yourself 71

Week 4 – Be Prayerful 75
   Day 1 – The Forgotten Power of Prayer..........................77
   Day 2 – Pray for Your Church..81

Day 3 – Pray for Your Pastor Search Committee 85
Day 4 – Pray for Your Next Pastor 91
Day 5 – Pray for Your Next Pastor's Family 95

Week 5 – Be Patient 99
Day 1 – The Need for Patience...................................... 101
Day 2 – The Setup Phase... 105
Day 3 – The Study Phase 109
Day 4 – The Search Phase.. 113
Day 5 – The Select and Support Phases...................... 117

Week 6 – Be Productive...123
Day 1 – The Church Is Still the Church...................... 125
Day 2 – Fruit Inspection... 129
Day 3 – Abide in Christ... 133
Day 4 – Gifted to Serve... 137
Day 5 – The Mission Continues 141

Small-Group Leader Guide 147

About the Author... 157

Congregational Covenant 158

Acknowledgments

This book has been both a burden and a dream of mine for a long time. It has been a burden because I have witnessed so many churches endure some of their most challenging days while they are without a pastor. It has been a dream because of a desire to help not only the churches in my Association, but other churches as well. Because of some incredible folks, this dream has now become a reality.

To my wife, Brandi, thank you for your understanding and support throughout this project. Thanks for patiently listening as I shared chapter ideas, potential covers, and so many other details. I'm incredibly grateful to the Lord for giving me such a wonderful helper in the ministry. I love you more than words can say.

To my friend and colleague David Stokes, thank you for your encouragement throughout this project and for reviewing the earliest drafts of the manuscript and offering invaluable feedback. I appreciate your support in so many ways, but I'm most thankful for your friendship and the investments you've made in my life and ministry.

To my pastor, John Lucas, thank you for your flexibility in helping me balance two ministry roles for the past five years. It has been one of my greatest joys in ministry to serve alongside you at First Baptist Church. As I have told you many times, I have no doubt God has called you to serve for such a time as this. Thank you for being my pastor and one of my best friends.

To Jim Altman, thank you for giving me the idea for this book. It was an incredible honor to serve as your interim pastor for a season and to help your church during the search. I hope the finished product is what you had in mind!

To Jeremiah Zeiset and the team at Aneko Press, thank you for your diligence in guiding me through the publication process. You have made this experience simple and as painless as possible. I truly appreciate your support!

To all my ministry colleagues who read portions of the manuscript and offered encouraging feedback, thank you for taking the time to review this material. I pray this book will become an indispensable resource for you as you help churches search for their next pastor.

To the churches of the Pike Association of Southern Baptists, it has been an honor to serve with you for the past seven years as we have sought to partner together to reach eastern Kentucky and the world for Christ. Thank you for allowing me to walk alongside so many of you as you have searched for your next pastor.

Finally, to you, the reader, thank you for taking an

active role in your church's search. It is my prayer that this book will encourage you and your fellow church members in this season of transition. You may or may not be involved in the nuts and bolts of the search, but regardless, your role is still extremely important. By seeking to honor Christ in your attitudes and behaviors, you can make a tremendous difference for your church during the search.

To my wife, Brandi:
God gave me much more than I
deserve when He gave me you.
Thanks for taking this
incredible journey with me.

To our sons, Isaiah and Noah:
It is one of the greatest privileges
of my life to be your Daddy.
Work hard. Play hard. Honor God.
I love you all.

Introduction

It seemed like a normal Sunday. Mark woke up early and made a cup of coffee. After reading his Bible and taking a shower, he, along with his wife, Jessica, somehow managed to get their three kids fed, dressed, and in the van just in time for Sunday school. Praise the Lord for small victories!

Mark and Jessica had been members at First Baptist Church for six years. Mark began teaching an adult couples class at the church last summer with the hope of reaching other young families like his own. The class had grown substantially since then.

After Sunday school, the couple picked up their children from their classes and walked to the sanctuary for the worship service. Although their Sunday school class attendance was lower than usual, the worship attendance seemed higher. As they scanned the outdated sanctuary, they spotted a young family that had recently moved into the neighborhood. Jessica had dropped off a dessert soon after the family had unloaded the moving truck, and she had become fast friends with Elizabeth, a wife and mom of two preschoolers. Mark and Jessica had been praying and inviting the family to their church for several weeks, and they were excited to see they had finally accepted the invitation. As they squeezed onto the pew with their new neighbors, the service began.

Pastor Larry welcomed everyone and shared a few announcements. The local homeless shelter was running low on canned green beans, parents of the youth group needed to meet after the service to discuss summer camp, and there would be a new women's Bible study beginning this Tuesday morning.

After the announcements, John led the congregation in several songs. John was an older gentleman in the church, and he had been the volunteer worship leader for more than twenty years. After the singing and the collection of the offering, Pastor Larry preached a shorter sermon than usual. He also seemed a little distracted as he stumbled over his words a few times during the message. That wasn't like him.

During the invitation, several of the deacons went up to the altar and prayed. After praying, the deacon chairman rose and gave Pastor Larry a brief hug before returning to his seat. Once the invitation was over, Pastor Larry stepped back behind the pulpit and asked everyone to sit down.

The next few minutes were a blur. Mark and Jessica sat in stunned silence as Pastor Larry announced he was resigning as pastor, effective in two weeks. They were devastated. They had joined First Baptist Church after meeting Pastor Larry at their oldest son's baseball game. His son was the same age as their son, and he had invited them to church. After Mark's father had passed away, they began attending regularly. A few months later, in their living room, Pastor Larry led both Mark and Jessica to trust in Jesus Christ. He baptized them the following Sunday.

Now he was leaving, and they didn't know what would happen next.

The details may change, but you can probably relate. If you're reading this book, it's likely due to the fact that your church will be without a pastor in the not-so-distant future. Maybe your pastor has recently announced his resignation, or perhaps he's already gone. The bottom line is his tenure is in the past, and you're facing an uncertain future.

While most books on this subject are written to train and equip the church leaders who will actually conduct the search for a new pastor, there are few resources written with you, the church member, in mind. This book is meant to fill that void.

My goal is to help you and your fellow church members navigate this season of transition. I want to help you deal with the emotions of saying goodbye to one pastor and preparing to say hello to a new one. I want to provide you with a general understanding of the activities taking place behind the scenes. Most importantly, I want to encourage you to honor the Lord during these uncertain days.

Six Commitments You'll Need to Make

Many years ago, in what now seems like a galaxy far, far away, I was an athlete. I wasn't the best player on the roster, but I wasn't the worst either. At least I didn't think so. That all changed when I was twelve years old and had been picked to be on my Little League All-Star baseball team. After several weeks of practice in hot and humid conditions, the coach told us everyone would have a chance to play in our first game. And everyone did – except me.

I wish I could say I took it all in stride, but that's not true. I wanted to quit. I wanted to forget about the countless hours of batting and fielding practice. Who cares about all the work I had put in? If I was going to sit the bench, why bother? But just before the next game, I overheard a conversation between my mom and her brother, and I'll never forget my uncle's words. He said, "Don't teach your son to be a quitter." In other words, I had made a commitment to my teammates, and I needed to honor that commitment.

Throughout this season of transition, there will be things that encourage you, and there will probably be things that frustrate you. During those frustrating moments, you might be tempted to throw in the towel. But if you're going to make the most of this interim period, you and your fellow church members will need to stay firmly committed to the Lord and to each other.

In fact, in my experience, I have found that there are six specific commitments you'll need to make in order to ensure that this will be a positive season in the life of your church. Over the course of the next six weeks, we're going to examine each of these commitments in greater detail. Here's a quick preview of where we're headed:

Commitment #1: Be Prepared

During this season of transition, there will be certain scenarios that your church will experience. There will be times when you don't know who will be preaching on Sunday. There will be times when circumstances don't go as planned. There will be times when you don't hear any news from the Pastor Search Committee. Week 1 will explain the reasons why these things happen and will suggest ways for you to respond whenever they do. Since you know you will likely experience all these scenarios in the coming days, now is the time to prepare.

Commitment #2: Be Informed

Every church member has a different opinion regarding the characteristics of a good pastor. While everyone is entitled to their opinion, it's imperative that you and your fellow church members develop a biblical understanding of how God defines pastoral faithfulness. During this week, we'll examine the biblical roles and qualifications of a pastor so you and your fellow church members will have an informed understanding of what your Search Committee needs to look for.

Commitment #3: Be Humble

In Philippians 2:1-4, the apostle Paul tells the church he had started earlier in his ministry to *make my joy*

complete. The way they were to do so was to be unified and to put the interests (or preferences) of others
above their own. As you know, this is much easier said
than done. During Week 3, we'll discuss different ways
church members are tempted to selfishly pursue their
own interests during the search and how you can avoid
giving in to those temptations.

Commitment #4: Be Prayerful

One of the activities during an interim period that is
often mentioned, but often overlooked, is intentional
times of prayer. However, congregational prayer is
essential for the church during the search. Throughout
this week, you'll be challenged to commit to frequent
and fervent times of prayer, both individually and
corporately. You will also learn practical ways to pray
for your church, your Pastor Search Committee, your
next pastor, and your next pastor's family. Remember
– churches that pray together stay together!

Commitment #5: Be Patient

One of the biggest mistakes Pastor Search Committees
make is rushing the search process. This often happens
because the committee feels the pressure of anxious
church members who pepper them with questions or
complaints about the length of the process. Given the
fact that the average search process takes twelve to
eighteen months, you must commit to be patient and
allow the Search Committee to do their work without
ongoing congregational nagging. During this week, we

will cover the five phases of the Pastor Search Process and explain why your patience is so vital to the process.

Commitment #6: Be Productive

The church is *still* the church, even when the office of pastor is vacant. However, church members are often tempted to slack off in their church commitments during an interim period. Church attendance sometimes wanes. However, every member is part of the body of Christ and has a role to fill. If they fail to do so, the whole body suffers (1 Corinthians 12). Therefore, this final week will encourage you to commit to being "all in" during the time when your church may need you the most.

Your Role in the Search

As you work through these pages, I hope you'll discover that you have an indispensable role in your church's search. God does not intend for you to sit idly by on the sidelines while you wait for your next pastor. You have the ability to make things much easier or much more difficult for those assigned that responsibility.

So let me encourage you to embrace your role by making these six commitments. If you're willing to do so, you will honor the Lord in your attitudes and behaviors during the search. If you or your fellow church members are unwilling to do so, difficult days are almost certainly on the horizon.

To assist you in taking an active role in the process, there's a section at the end of each daily reading called "Your Role in the Search." In it you will find three components:

- **Review:** This is a brief summary of the main point of each daily reading. It will help you to remember the contents of the reading in the future.

- **Reflect:** This is a question to help you further process the content from the daily reading. Let me encourage you to not simply *think* about these reflection questions, but to actually *write* out your answers in the margin or in a separate journal.

- **Respond:** Each daily reading will conclude with a suggested Bible passage for further study or a specific prayer recommendation for the purpose of applying the topic to your life and your church.

Individual or Group Study

As mentioned earlier, this book is designed to be studied over the course of six weeks. Each week includes five daily readings that focus on one of the six commitments. It can be studied by individuals or in a small-group setting.

If you choose individual study only, you can read through the readings at your own pace, although I still recommend that you read one per day for thirty days. Several topics will require substantial thought and self-reflection, and limiting yourself to only one per day will allow adequate time to do so.

For those who would like to discuss the material

with others, it's recommended that you complete the five daily readings before each group session. There is a seven-week Leader Guide included in the appendix (with an optional introductory session) to assist in your group meetings.

If you are leading a group through this material, you will find several resources including videos, additional discussion questions, and other resources at **churchsearchbook.com/smallgroups**.

Let's Begin

I know you don't know what the future holds for your church, but I know who holds the future, and Jesus has promised never to leave or forsake you (Joshua 1:5; Hebrews 13:5). He will help you and your fellow church members get through these difficult days and come out spiritually stronger on the other side.

With this confident expectation, let's begin this journey as we learn together how to be the church during the search!

Week 1 – Be Prepared

During this season of transition, you will encounter different scenarios. There will be times when you don't know who's preaching on Sunday. There will be times when things don't go as planned with the search. There will be times when you don't hear any news from the Pastor Search Committee. Knowing you will most likely experience all these scenarios, now is the time to prepare for how you will respond in those moments. This week's readings will show you how to do so.

What Just Happened?

There is an occasion for everything, and a time for every activity under heaven.
—Ecclesiastes 3:1

My first truck was a blue 1993 Ford Ranger. I loved that truck. My parents bought it for me during my senior year of high school, and I drove it during my college years. When I sat behind the wheel for the last time, Old Blue had traveled more than 139,000 miles.

During my final semester of college, I commuted two days a week from Richmond, Kentucky, to Lexington for a paid internship. As a broke college student, I had been unable to afford new tires – and I would soon live to regret it. On a cold and snowy February morning, I was on my way to Lexington when my truck suddenly slid sideways. During the next few seconds, I felt several impacts as I lost control.

As I would learn later, another car traveling the same

direction struck me in the driver's side door when my truck slid sideways, which propelled Old Blue more than twenty feet into the winter sky. After rolling on my top and going airborne a second time, my truck landed on the side of the interstate with so much force that it broke off both rear axles. My wheels were found one hundred feet away, yet God protected me, and I walked away without a scratch!

Of course, I learned those details later. In the immediate moments after the accident, I was in shock. All I could do was ask, "What just happened?"

You may be asking that same question right now. While hopefully not as violent, the resignation of a pastor can be a traumatic experience, especially if you didn't see it coming. You might still be reeling from the news and not yet be able to process what this means for you and your church in the days ahead.

While the details surrounding your pastor's resignation are unique, you and your fellow church members are now facing what millions of other Christians have faced before you. If you have been a church member for more than a few years, this might not even be the first time you have experienced a season without a pastor.

As Solomon wrote in Ecclesiastes 3:1, there is a season for everything. Right now, you're in a season of transition. But, Lord willing, it will *only* be a season.

William Bridges explains that every transition has three stages,[1] and pastoral transitions are no different. First, there's an ending. Your previous pastor's tenure

---

1   William Bridges, *Transitions: Making Sense of Life's Changes* (Cambridge, MA: Da Capo Press, 2004), 4.

has come to a close. Regardless of how long his tenure lasted, members of your church (including you) probably responded to the news of his departure in one of four ways. Some members of your church were *mad* when they heard the news. Others were probably *sad*. Another group might have been *glad*. A few might have simply been *indifferent*. Depending on how recently your pastor resigned, there might be some people in the church still dealing with these emotions. If this describes you, keep in mind that it is normal to feel the way you do, but the day will soon come when you'll need to turn the page and begin to look to the future.

The middle stage is what Bridges calls "the neutral zone." In church life, it's known as "the interim period." This is the time between your previous pastor's ending and your new pastor's beginning. It's the time when your church will form a Pastor Search Committee and begin the search for a new pastor. It's also a time when churches often place many of their ministries on pause until the next pastor arrives. It's a time when some slack off in their attendance and service to the Lord. It can be a time of great difficulty, but it can also be a time of great opportunity. And it's the time that your church is in right now.

The final stage of transition is the new beginning when your new pastor arrives. During the first year, your church will experience a lot of firsts. There will be the first time you meet the new pastor and his family, the first time he preaches, the first time he conducts a baptism, the first time he leads the church to observe the Lord's Supper, the first time he conducts a wedding, the first time he conducts a funeral, the first time he participates in a business meeting, the first time he makes a hospital visit, the first Christmas message, the first Easter message, the first mistake, and so on. Over time, these firsts will become seconds and thirds, and eventually, you'll get used to the new normal for your church – and the season of transition will be over.

But for now, you're in the midst of this season. The good news is there is never a season when the Lord is not with you. He has promised to never leave or forsake you (Hebrews 13:5), and He will see you safely through this time. So trust in Him!

Your Role in the Search

- **Review:** Your church is in a season of transition, but it is only a season.

- **Reflect:** How did you feel when you found out your church would need to search for a new pastor? Were you mad, sad, glad, or indifferent? Why?

- **Respond:** Read Deuteronomy 31:1-23. In a journal, record any observations about the transition of leadership from Moses to Joshua.

Day 2

Who's Preaching Sunday?

For it has been reported to me about you, my brothers and sisters, by members of Chloe's people, that there is rivalry among you. What I am saying is this: One of you says, "I belong to Paul," or "I belong to Apollos," or "I belong to Cephas," or "I belong to Christ." Is Christ divided?
—1 Corinthians 1:11-13

*W*ho's preaching Sunday? For a time, you knew the answer to that question. You may or may not know the answer now. However, someone in your church should know. In fact, during the early days of the interim period, this will be your church's most pressing need. Sunday is always coming, and someone in your church has been assigned the responsibility to make sure that the pulpit is filled every week. It could be the deacons, the personnel committee, or another individual or group.

Those who have been assigned the task of considering potential preachers may choose to invite other pastors on staff to preach (if applicable), other church members, or they may reach out to the local association or denominational entity for a list of names of men who might be available. You might know some of the men who preach during the next few months, and you might not be familiar with others. You might enjoy listening to some more than others too!

Essentially, your church has two options for pulpit supply during the interim period. One option is to invite a variety of men to preach. While this provides the opportunity for you to hear someone different each week, this method places a heavier burden on those who are responsible for making sure the pulpit is filled. Coordinating multiple schedules will present challenges at times, and the church may be forced to scramble at the last minute to find someone to preach.

A second option is to secure an interim pastor. This option provides consistency in the pulpit and eases the transition from your former pastor to your next pastor. Given the fact that the average pastor search takes between twelve and eighteen months, securing an interim pastor may be preferable – if your church can find a qualified man who senses a calling to interim ministry. Regardless of which option your church pursues, the reality is that those who preach at your church during the next few months will do so on a temporary basis.

One of the dangers during the interim period is that

church members sometimes make the false assumption that everyone who preaches at your church is a candidate for the position. While this may be the case for some, it won't be the case for the majority. Most of the men who will preach at your church simply want to help in your time of need.

If everyone who preached during the interim period were candidates for the position, it would inevitably cause division among your congregation. Some would prefer one preacher, others would favor someone else, and still others would not want any of them.

Heed these words of caution. You may begin to prefer one preacher over others. You may be tempted to attend only when he is scheduled to preach. You may try to convince the Pastor Search Committee to select your favorite preacher as the next pastor. You may even be tempted to leave the church if the Search Committee doesn't listen to you. Don't give in to those temptations. Trust that the Lord is guiding your Pastor Search Committee to the man He is calling to be the next pastor – who may or may not be the man you prefer.

The Corinthian church found themselves in a similar situation. Some preferred Paul, others Apollos, and still others Cephas (1 Corinthians 1:12). But Paul makes the point that Christ is not divided, and His church shouldn't be either. He explains in 1 Corinthians 3:5-7: *What then is Apollos? What is Paul? They are servants through whom you believed, and each has the role the Lord has given. I planted, Apollos watered, but God gave the growth. So then neither the one who plants nor the one who waters is anything, but only God who gives the growth.*

A few verses later, he concludes: *So let no one boast in human leaders, for everything is yours – whether Paul or Apollos or Cephas or the world or life or death or things present or things to come – everything is yours, and you belong to Christ, and Christ belongs to God* (1 Corinthians 3:21-23).

In your church's current situation, the application is clear. Who will preach this Sunday at your church is not as important as who they are preaching about! If the gospel of Jesus Christ is proclaimed by the preacher, and if it is obeyed by the congregation, that is what matters most.

Your Role in the Search

- **Review:** Those who preach during the interim period are there to help, not to divide your church.

- **Reflect:** Read 1 Corinthians 1-4. How do these chapters apply to your church's current situation?

- **Respond:** What practical steps will you take to make sure your church involvement won't be determined by whoever is preaching each Sunday?

Day 3

When There Is No News

That's why all of you have conspired against me! Nobody tells me when my own son makes a covenant with Jesse's son. None of you cares about me or tells me that my son has stirred up my own servant to wait in ambush for me, as is the case today.
—1 Samuel 22:8

My kids think I grew up in the Dark Ages. Here's a recent conversation about the lack of technology available during my childhood:

Me: No computer.
Kids: *No thanks.*
Me: No Wi-Fi.
Kids: *Are you kidding me?*
Me: No cell phones.
Kids: *How did you live???*

My kids are amazed when I explain that we survived before the internet was invented. But still, I am a fan of modern technology. I remember one occasion when a cell phone would have reduced my stress level considerably.

My parents had traveled to a medical appointment 150 miles away, and they had planned to be back home around 6:00 p.m. However, the entire state was slammed with a massive snowstorm during the afternoon. Within a few hours, there was six inches of snow on the ground, with more to come. When 6:00 p.m. rolled around, there was no sign of my parents. At 7:00 p.m., still no parents. The same at 8:00 p.m.

You can understand the panic as a twelve-year-old boy begins to imagine different scenarios for why his parents had not yet arrived home. *Their car broke down and they have frozen to death. They slid off the road and drove over a cliff. They decided it was too bad to travel, and I'll be home alone tonight.* All these options terrified me. With no cell phone to check on them while they were traveling, I had no way to calm these fears. It was excruciating.

Finally, around 9:00 p.m., I saw headlights in the driveway. Sure enough, Mom and Dad were home, safe and sound. The only thing my worrying accomplished was to ruin my evening.

It's amazing how quickly we imagine worst-case scenarios whenever we don't have all the facts about a particular situation. During the coming months, there are going to be several times when you don't hear any news about how the pastor search is progressing. Read that last sentence again. There are going to be *several* times when you don't hear *any* news about how the pastor search is progressing.

When that happens, don't work yourself up over imagined scenarios. You might begin to imagine that the Search Committee is lazy and not doing anything. You might imagine they are incompetent. You might even imagine the committee has ulterior motives and is intentionally trying to keep secrets from the church. I know it's hard to avoid filling in the blanks with your best guess whenever you don't know all the answers, but if you're unable to fight that temptation, you are setting yourself up for several unnecessary headaches.

You might remember the account of King Saul and how he believed that David had led everyone to conspire against him. Absolutely convinced of this conspiracy, Saul went so far as to order the execution of eighty-five priests who he believed were assisting David in his supposed overthrow attempt (1 Samuel 22). There was much needless bloodshed simply because of one man who had connected dots in his mind that weren't meant to be connected. Don't make that same mistake.

The reality is there are legitimate reasons for why there might not be any news. As we will see later, there are several phases of a Pastor Search Process, and each phase can take a considerable amount of time. For example, the résumé collection process might remain open for several months. Therefore, the Search Committee might not be able to share any new updates simply because there are no new updates.

Another reason could be due to confidentiality. In the social-media age, all it takes is one church member to comment on a potential candidate's Facebook page to cause many problems for him. If his current church members were to find out there's a possibility he might be leaving, the consequences could be devastating, especially if God is not calling him to your church. He would then be forced to have difficult conversations with his church that could have been avoided.

Therefore, in order to protect the confidentiality of potential candidates, there might be times when the Search Committee cannot share any new information with you or your fellow church members.

The Pastor Search Process will have many ups and downs. There will be leads and there will be dead ends. There will be times of great encouragement and times of great discouragement. There will be times when it seems that the process is moving quickly, and there will be other times when it seems to move at a snail's pace. But you probably won't know most of that because it will be going on behind the scenes.

Therefore, whenever there is no news, let me encourage you to give the Search Committee the benefit of the doubt. Instead of spending time second-guessing them, why not spend that time praying for them? Their task is incredibly important and incredibly difficult; they desperately need your prayers and support. More on that topic later!

Your Role in the Search

- **Review:** There are legitimate reasons why you may not hear updates at times.

- **Reflect:** You've probably heard the saying, "Perception is reality." What are some ways your perception might be different than the reality of the pastor search?

- **Respond:** Read 1 Samuel 22 and ask the Lord to help you avoid following Saul's example during your church's search for a new pastor.

Day 4

When Things Don't Go as Planned

We know that all things work together for the good of those who love God, who are called according to his purpose.
—Romans 8:28

I'm the type of guy who likes to have a plan. When I wake up, I open my daily planner and plan my day. Before we go on vacation, I create a plan for how our family will spend our time. When I go grocery shopping, I have a plan for how to get in and out as quickly as possible.

Needless to say, I became frustrated during the spring of 2020 when the global coronavirus pandemic obliterated all my plans. I had planned on going on spring break with my family. That didn't happen. I had planned on a packed church house on Easter Sunday. The building sat empty and quiet. I had planned on my beloved Kentucky Wildcats cutting down the nets after winning their ninth national championship. Sadly, that didn't happen either.

The global pandemic of 2020 threw a monkey wrench into everyone's plans. Nothing went as planned for months, and it left us all frustrated, angry, depressed, and worried at times. The list of emotions appeared to be endless.

The reality is that the Pastor Search Process can also be full of surprises. One thing is for certain: things will not always go as planned. Consider these true stories:

- The committee at one church had narrowed their search to a single candidate. After announcing he would be presented to the church the following Sunday for a vote, the candidate withdrew his name from consideration, and the committee had to start over.

- In another church, the congregation voted down three different candidates before the entire Pastor Search Committee resigned.

- Another Search Committee ended talks with their top candidate after a pattern of questionable behavior was discovered during the reference checks.

- In another church, the committee's top candidate was called as pastor. After six weeks, he abruptly resigned, and the congregation was devastated.

- A small church located in a rural setting struggled for more than two years to receive interest from any candidates.

I could go on, but you get the idea. Your church and your Pastor Search Committee will undoubtedly develop a plan for how to conduct the search for your next pastor. However, those plans are subject to change. The Bible teaches that God is sovereign, which means that He is in control. Proverbs 16:9 says, *A person's heart plans his way, but the LORD determines his steps.* In Ephesians 1:11, Paul writes that God *works out everything in agreement with the purpose of his will.* In Romans 8:28, Paul writes that *all things work together for the good of those who love God, who are called according to his purpose.*

In other words, our plans are subject to change based upon God's plans, and pastor searches are not exempt from this biblical truth. Expect the unexpected.

Whenever things don't go as planned, you might experience emotions similar to what I felt during the pandemic. You might be frustrated, angry, depressed, or worried. You might even look for someone to blame. These responses are quite common, but I believe there is a better way to respond.

If you prepare yourself to expect the unexpected during the search, you'll be more likely to respond with grace and understanding in those surprise moments. Nobody's perfect. No plan is perfect. If God chooses to change the plan, who are we to complain about it (Romans 9:20-21)?

Furthermore, when things don't go as planned, there will be no one more disappointed than the Pastor Search Committee. Rather than complaining or criticizing them, it is during these surprise moments that they most need to be encouraged. You can be that agent of encouragement. Let them know how much you appreciate their efforts. Let them know how much you are praying for them. Let them know you love and support them. The sooner the committee overcomes their discouragement, the sooner they can get back on track. So let me say it again: *be an agent of encouragement.*

Your Role in the Search

- **Review:** There will be times when the search doesn't go as planned.

- **Reflect:** How do you respond when your plans are changed?

- **Respond:** You don't have to wait for surprises before you start encouraging your Pastor Search Committee. Make a list of creative ways you can begin encouraging the committee right now.

Day 5

The Elephant in the Room

Don't you know that those who perform the temple services eat the food from the temple, and those who serve at the altar share in the offerings of the altar? In the same way, the Lord has commanded that those who preach the gospel should earn their living by the gospel.
—1 Corinthians 9:13-14

Ah, yes. The elephant in the room – a difficult topic that everyone knows about but no one wants to mention or discuss because it's uncomfortable to do so. I'm sure you've noticed an elephant or two in the past. The forty-year-old who still lives with his parents is the elephant in the room at family gatherings. Your friend's bad haircut is the elephant in the room during dinner. The soloist who doesn't have any vocal talent is the elephant in the room during the worship service. You get the idea.

When it comes to the church during the search, your elephant in the room will most likely be your next pastor's salary. It is an uncomfortable topic because money is often misunderstood from a biblical standpoint. There is the time when Jesus taught His disciples to store up treasures in heaven rather than on earth (Matthew 6:19-21). A few verses later, He taught that you cannot serve both God and money (Matthew 6:24). Then there's Paul declaring that *the love of money is a root of all kinds of evil* (1 Timothy 6:10). It's no wonder most church members think that the pastor's salary is a discussion to avoid at all costs. Because that's the case, confusion about the topic is common among church members.

However, as Paul states in 1 Corinthians 9:14, *The Lord has commanded that those who preach the gospel should earn their living by the gospel.* In other words, your church can't avoid this topic. You must be prepared to address the elephant in the room. It will save your church and your next pastor potential headaches later on.

Although it's a necessary discussion, that does not mean it's an easy discussion. Adding to the confusion is the fact that it is often unclear exactly how much the pastor will be paid. The reason for this is that churches usually offer a pastor a "pay package" that includes the pastor's salary, housing allowance, retirement benefits, health insurance, conference and automobile reimbursements, and utilities paid by the church. This is the total that the pastor will cost the church. For illustration purposes, let's say that comes out to $60,000. If you were to ask most of the members of your church, they would say your pastor makes $60,000 per year.

But that's an incorrect statement. In reality, the pastor makes much less. In the example above, it's likely that his salary is closer to $40,000. Think of it this way. If I were to ask you how much money you made, you would tell me your annual salary. You would probably balk if I suggested we should add the cost your employer pays for your health insurance to the calculation. Similarly, you would hesitate if I suggested that we add your employer's retirement contributions to the total. You would probably think I was crazy to suggest you should also include any reimbursements you received for business travel. But that's what church members do when they say their pastor makes $60,000 as in the example above.

The truth is there's a big difference between a pay package and a salary. Churches often confuse the two. The total compensation package is the total cost to the church, but that's not the same thing as the pastor's salary. Later in the search process, you will be asked to vote on a proposed compensation package. When you do so, make sure you know how much of the package is salary and how much is composed of other benefits.

Also, when the compensation package is presented, it's likely those numbers won't materialize out of thin air. There are a number of resources available to your church leaders to help them develop a salary and benefits package comparable to churches of similar size, budget, and location. These resources help to make sure your pastor will not be underpaid.

Speaking of underpaying your pastor, Thom Rainer writes that most ministers are underpaid.[2] In fact, more than 80 percent of pastors surveyed said they felt financial burdens.[3] In light of this fact, your church should strive to be as generous as possible in order to ease any concerns that your pastor's family will not be well supplied. If you can ease these concerns, your pastor can focus his energies on shepherding the flock. In other words, if you'll do everything you can to take care of your next pastor and his family, he will do everything he can to take care of you.

Finally, you might be in a small church that cannot afford a full-time pastor. If so, you're not alone. More than half the churches in my Association are served by bi-vocational pastors who have a second source of income in order to provide for their families. If your church is in a similar situation, you can still strive to be as generous as possible.

A pastor's salary is not usually a comfortable topic for the church or potential candidates. However, your church needs to be prepared to discuss the elephant in the room. Talk through it now so you can be as generous as possible later.

---

2   Thom Rainer with Art Rainer, "The Minister's Salary," www.mbfoundation.com/wp-content/uploads/2014/10/2014-The-Ministers-Salary.pdf, 4.

3   Rainer, 4.

Your Role in the Search

- **Review:** Your church has a biblical responsibility to provide for your pastor and his family as much as possible.

- **Reflect:** Why do you think churches sometimes confuse a pastor's salary and his pay package? What steps can your church take to avoid this confusion in the future?

- **Respond:** Read 1 Corinthians 9:1-18, taking special note of the number of times Paul speaks about the church's responsibility to provide for its pastor(s).

Week 2 – Be Informed

Every church member has a different opinion regarding the characteristics of a good pastor. While everyone is entitled to their opinion, it is imperative that you and your fellow church members develop a biblical understanding of how God defines pastoral faithfulness. During this week, we will examine the biblical roles and qualifications of a pastor so you and your fellow church members will have an *informed* understanding of what your Search Committee needs to look for.

Day 1

Shepherds Feed the Flock

Man must not live on bread alone but on every word that comes from the mouth of God.
—Matthew 4:4

f you were to look up the word "pastor" in the New
Testament, you wouldn't find it often in most English
translations. In fact, in a few translations, you wouldn't
find it all! However, most translations include the word
one time in Ephesians 4:11-12: *And [Christ] gave some
to be apostles, some prophets, some evangelists, some
pastors and teachers, equipping the saints for the work
of ministry, to build up the body of Christ* (emphasis
added).

The Greek word for "pastor" is *poimēn*, and it is used
seventeen times in the Greek New Testament. In all
other instances it is translated as "shepherd" – because
that's what a pastor is. He is the spiritual shepherd in a

local church, serving under the authority of the Chief Shepherd, Jesus Christ.

Therefore, in order to gain a proper understanding of God's expectations for your next pastor, you must understand what it means for him to serve as your spiritual shepherd. From the well-known Psalm 23, it's clear that shepherds fulfill at least four tasks: shepherds feed, lead, protect, and comfort their flocks. Let's begin today to examine the first of these tasks in greater detail.

One of the primary duties of a shepherd is to provide food, shelter, and rest for his sheep. As the first three verses of Psalm 23 explain, that's what God does for us as our Chief Shepherd: *The LORD is my shepherd; I have what I need. He lets me lie down in green pastures; he leads me beside quiet waters. He renews my life.*

When David writes, *I have what I need*, he means that the sheep will not lack what is needed because the shepherd provides for the sheep. Green pastures provide ample opportunities for food. Quiet waters provide a safe place to drink. These verses show that God provides for our needs, both physically (Matthew 6:25-33) and spiritually.

As Jesus taught in Matthew 4:4, our spiritual food comes from the Word of God. As a Christian, you are certainly expected to read and feed on God's Word on your own on a regular basis. Jesus said in John 8:31, *If you continue in my word, you really are my disciples.* In addition to your personal reading and study of the Bible, God has provided undershepherds to help you understand it. In Jeremiah 3:15 (ESV) we read, *I will give you shepherds after my own heart, who will feed you with knowledge and understanding.*

Therefore, it is the biblical duty and responsibility of your pastor to spiritually feed you with a regular diet of God's Word. That's why Paul commands his protégé Timothy to *preach the word* (2 Timothy 4:2).

So what does this mean for you as a member of the flock of God? Here is a rule of thumb I had as a kid and my kids now have: *Most things that taste good aren't good for you, and many things that don't taste good are good for you.*

If you were to ask me to choose between an Oreo Blizzard or a full plate of brussels sprouts, I'm going for the Blizzard every time! But a regular diet of Oreo Blizzards is not going to end well. You and I need proper nutrition to remain healthy. This is true physically as well as spiritually.

Therefore, if your next pastor provides a regular diet of God's Word, it might not always "taste" good, but it will be good for you. The writer of Hebrews explains: *For the word of God is living and effective and sharper than any double-edged sword, penetrating as far as the separation of soul and spirit, joints and marrow. It is able to judge the thoughts and intentions of the heart* (Hebrews 4:12). Again, it won't always feel good, but it's good for you!

If your pastor is faithfully fulfilling this task of feeding his flock, he will preach on biblical passages and topics that may step on your toes from time to time. He will preach on subjects that make you uncomfortable. He will preach from texts that will be confusing and hard to understand. When those times come, don't refuse to eat or try to spit it back out. Receive the food from the shepherd so that you will be spiritually healthy. As you maintain a healthy and balanced spiritual diet from God's Word, you will continue to grow in your faith.

Your Role in the Search

- **Review:** As your spiritual shepherd, your pastor will have a responsibility to feed you a well-balanced diet from God's Word.

- **Reflect:** What type of spiritual diet have you grown accustomed to? Do you feed on Oreo Blizzards or brussels sprouts – or a combination of both?

- **Respond:** Begin to pray today that your next pastor will be faithful to teach and preach the whole counsel of God and that you and your fellow church members will receive it with glad and generous hearts.

Shepherds Lead the Flock

May the LORD, the God who gives breath to all, appoint a man over the community who will go out before them and come back in before them, and who will bring them out and bring them in, so that the LORD's community won't be like sheep without a shepherd.
—Numbers 27:16-17

As a child, I loved playing the game called "follow the leader." If it has been a while since you've played it, I'll refresh your memory. First, a leader is chosen and the rest of the children line up behind the leader. The leader then moves around, and the followers have to mimic the leader's actions. Any child who fails to follow or do what the leader does is out of the game. When only one person other than the leader remains, that child is declared the winner. That player becomes the leader, and the game begins again with all players following the new leader.

If you know anything about sheep, you know they would be the champions of "follow the leader." They always follow their shepherd. Wherever he goes, the sheep are right behind him. That's what sheep do; they follow their leader.

Notice also that the shepherd leads the sheep from the front. He doesn't attempt to drive them forward from the back. He leads from the front because he knows where he's going. The sheep have no idea what's up ahead, and they don't need to know. The sheep may not know where the green pastures are, but the shepherd does. The sheep may not know where the still waters are, but the shepherd does. All they need to do is to follow the shepherd because he knows where he is going.

What a comforting reminder for Christians today! Several times in Psalm 23:1-3 we see how God leads us: He makes us lie down in green pastures, He leads us beside still waters, and He leads us in paths of righteousness. We are the flock of God; He leads us, and He expects us to follow.

Just as the Lord appoints His undershepherds to feed His flocks on His behalf, He also appoints them to lead His flocks on His behalf. In Numbers 27:16-17, God told Moses to climb the mountain to see the promised land, informing him that he would then die. If I were Moses, I probably would have been devastated by this news. I may have thrown a pity party for myself. But not Moses. The first thing he did after receiving this news was to ask the Lord to appoint another man to lead the congregation in his place. That's a shepherd's heart!

God responded to Moses' request by appointing Joshua as the new leader. He instructed Moses, *Confer some of your authority on him so that the entire community will obey him* (Numbers 27:20). Further, *all the Israelites with [Joshua], even the entire community, will go out and come back in at his command* (Numbers 27:21). God gave Joshua the authority to lead and the expectation that the congregation would follow his leadership.

Similarly, when you call your next pastor, God will appoint him to lead this flock on His behalf during the next season in the life of your church. He will grant him the authority to lead and will give you the responsibility to follow.

This does *not* mean he should lead in a manner that is forceful or manipulative. Also, God has not given him the authority to lead the church to sin in any way. Instead, he is to lead according to God's instructions in 1 Peter 5:2-3: *Shepherd God's flock among you, not overseeing out of compulsion but willingly, as God would have you; not out of greed for money but eagerly; nor lording it over those entrusted to you, but being examples to the flock.*

Your new pastor will not be a perfect leader. The only perfect leader was Jesus (2 Corinthians 5:21). But if he attempts to lead in a 1 Peter 5 way, you have an obligation to follow his leadership. That doesn't mean you will always understand or agree with every decision he makes, but it does mean you will need to trust that God has appointed him to lead and wants you to follow.

Your Role in the Search

- **Review:** As your spiritual shepherd, your pastor will have a God-given responsibility to lead your church.

- **Reflect:** How have you responded to pastoral leadership in the past? Do you usually follow the leader, or do you try to follow your own path?

- **Respond:** Based upon today's reading, how might your disposition toward pastoral leadership need to change?

Day 3

Shepherds Protect the Flock

I know that after my departure savage wolves will come in among you, not sparing the flock.
—Acts 20:29

In Judah, the valleys in the desert often cast deep shadows, and you never know what might be lurking in those shadows. There might be bandits, predators, or even flash floods, all of which were dangerous threats to the flock. Those valleys are what David speaks of when he says he walks *through the valley of the shadow of death* (Psalm 23:4 ESV). The valley can be a dangerous place for the sheep.

But David continues: *Even though I walk through the valley of the shadow of death, I will fear no evil.* Why is he not afraid? Because his Shepherd is with him. You see, another role of a shepherd is to protect his sheep from danger. His rod and staff comfort the sheep because the shepherd can use them as defensive weapons against anyone or anything that tries to attack the sheep. The sheep don't need to be afraid as long as their shepherd is present.

As our Good Shepherd, Jesus laid down His life to protect us from the greatest danger of all – the eternal consequences of our sin (John 10:11). He has also appointed undershepherds to protect the church from other dangers.

First, pastors are called to protect the flock from division. In Ephesians 4:1-3, Paul urges the church *to walk worthy of the calling you have received, with all humility and gentleness, with patience, bearing with one another in love, making every effort to keep the unity of the Spirit through the bond of peace.* A few verses later, he says that God has given pastors and teachers to the church in order *to equip the saints for the work of ministry, to build up the body of Christ, until we all reach unity in the faith* (Ephesians 4:12-13). Whenever divisions and conflicts arise in a church, pastors are given the responsibility to address them quickly in order to prevent a greater rift among God's people.

A second way pastors protect the flock is to protect them from sin. In Galatians 6:1, Paul writes, *Brothers and sisters, if someone is overtaken in any wrongdoing,* ***you who are spiritual****, restore such a person with a gentle spirit* (emphasis added). While this command doesn't apply only to pastors, it certainly includes them. Pastors must tend their flocks and warn them to wrestle with and overcome sin in all its forms.

One final way pastors protect their flocks is to protect them from false teaching. In Acts 20, Paul bids farewell to the Ephesian elders. As he does so, he warns them of imminent danger: *Be on guard for yourselves and for all the flock of which the Holy Spirit has appointed you as overseers, to shepherd the church of God, which he purchased with his own blood. I know that after my departure savage wolves will come in among you, not sparing the flock. Men will rise up even from your own number and distort the truth to lure the disciples into following them. Therefore be on the alert* (Acts 20:28-31).

Whenever a pastor seeks to protect the flock in these and other ways, it is not usually pleasant for him or the church, but it is a necessary part of his role. So what does this mean for you as a member of God's flock? It simply means you should embrace the protection of the shepherd and not fight against it.

Have you ever stopped a toddler from touching a hot stove? Have you maybe grabbed them right before they jumped into a swimming pool? You probably warned them not to do it again, but you had to stop them again a few minutes later. You have probably found that these young humans don't often appreciate your intervention. They might scream and cry. They might punch and kick. Sometimes they might even try to bite you – all because you are trying to protect them from danger.

Unfortunately, church members sometimes respond to their pastor the same way. The resistance may not be physical, but it's just as explosive. It might happen when he warns you to avoid a certain book or a particular online preacher because the teaching is contrary to Scripture, when he refuses to take sides in a church conflict and warns you not to get involved either, or when he calls you to repent of a certain sin in your life.

Each of these examples are pastoral attempts to protect the flock. Unfortunately, church members don't always respond positively to these protective measures. Sometimes they fight back and make false accusations against the pastor. Sometimes they yell at him. Sometimes they withhold their tithe. Sometimes they leave the church.

You don't have to be that person. Instead of fighting against your pastor's protective efforts, embrace them. Your next pastor will be a gift from the Lord to help shepherd your heart. Don't bite the shepherd; rest in the shadow of his protection instead!

Your Role in the Search

- **Review:** As your spiritual shepherd, your pastor will have a God-given responsibility to protect your church from dangers such as division, sin, and false teaching.

- **Reflect:** If your new pastor were to warn you that a particular preacher you listen to on the radio or online often teaches doctrines contrary to the Bible, how would you respond?

- **Respond:** Pray today that you would be sensitive to the protective efforts of your next pastor.

Shepherds Comfort the Flock

*For you are with me; your rod and your
staff – they comfort me.*
—Psalm 23:4

It was noted yesterday that the shepherd's rod and staff comfort the sheep. This might seem counterintuitive since the rod and staff could be used to discipline wayward sheep, but David doesn't see it that way. He doesn't view the rod and staff as a means of *concern*, but as a means of *comfort*. He is able to rest because he knows he's not alone. Someone who cares deeply for him is close by, and that is a comforting thought.

It should come as no surprise that God is described as the *God of all comfort, who comforts us in all our affliction* (2 Corinthians 1:3-4 ESV). The Bible teaches elsewhere that the Lord will never leave us nor forsake us (Hebrews 13:5), and that nothing can separate us from His love through Christ Jesus (Romans 8:39).

Even as you now find yourself without a pastor, the good news is you're not alone. Christ is still the head of your church (Colossians 1:18), and He's still right there with you (Matthew 28:20). What a comforting thought!

One of the primary ways the Lord comforts us during trying times is through the presence of other brothers and sisters. Paul goes on to say that the God of all comfort *comforts us in all our affliction, **so that we may be able to comfort those who are in any affliction**, with the comfort with which we ourselves are comforted by God* (2 Corinthians 1:4 ESV, emphasis added).

The body of Christ has been given many "one anothers" in Scripture. We are commanded to love one another (John 15:12), to serve one another (1 Peter 4:10), and to bear one another's burdens (Galatians 6:2). We are called to be devoted to one another (Romans 12:10), to honor one another (Romans 12:10), and to live in harmony with one another (Romans 12:16). We are called to forgive one another (Colossians 3:13), to exhort one another (Hebrews 3:13), and to pray for one another (James 5:16). The list goes on, but you get the picture. The command to comfort others is one of many ways the church ministers to one another, and during the darkest moments in our lives, God often comforts us through the presence of our pastor.

While the preaching of God's Word is the primary task of a pastor, it is not the only task. There is a difference between a preacher and a pastor. A pastor recognizes that sometimes the best thing he can do for a hurting church member is to *show up* and *shut up* – to simply be there, to weep with those who weep, to mourn with those who mourn, and to be a comforting presence in their time of trouble.

This means it is okay to want your pastor to be there for you during tough times. That's part of his calling. However, while it is okay to *desire* his presence, it is not okay to *demand* it. Your next pastor will be busy, just like you – and just like Jesus.

In the first chapter of Mark's gospel, we catch a glimpse of the busyness of Jesus' ministry. On this particular day, Jesus and His disciples entered Capernaum, and He went into the synagogue to teach. While He taught, a man with an unclean spirit interrupted Him. Jesus commanded the spirit to come out of the man, and to everyone's amazement, the spirit obeyed. After leaving the synagogue, they walked to Simon's house, and Jesus healed Simon's mother-in-law. Later that same evening, the whole town assembled at the door as Jesus healed many others who were sick with various diseases. He also drove out many demons (Mark 1:21-34).

Mark tells us that early the next morning, Jesus woke up and went out to a deserted place to pray. Simon and the other disciples searched for Him. When they found Him, they said, *Everyone is looking for you* (Mark 1:37). In other words, there were more people who needed Jesus to comfort them by healing or exorcism, and His disciples couldn't understand why He was alone in the desert. So many were hurting, so many needed a healing touch, so many needed to be comforted – and Jesus had the power to help them all.

Given the demands from the Capernaum residents, the disciples were probably surprised by Jesus' response.

He answered, *Let's go on to the neighboring villages so that I may preach there too* (Mark 1:38). Instead of returning to Simon's house to continue to comfort those in Capernaum, Jesus moved on to the next village. It meant that He left some needs unmet.

Apply this principle to your next pastor. Think about it: if Jesus could not be in two places at once during His earthly ministry, neither can your pastor. This means there *will be* times when your pastor can't be at the hospital to pray with you before your surgery. There *will be* times when he won't be available to counsel you during a challenging experience. During those times, know that your pastor still loves you and will do his best to comfort you in your time of trouble, even if it is not in the timing or way you would prefer.

Your Role in the Search

- **Review:** As your spiritual shepherd, your pastor will have a God-given responsibility to comfort you during your times of suffering as much as his time and ability will allow.

- **Reflect:** How have you been comforted by a former pastor or fellow church member?

- **Respond:** What are some practical ways you can help your next pastor comfort fellow church members who are going through difficult times?

Shepherds Must Be Qualified

*This saying is trustworthy: "If anyone
aspires to be an overseer, he desires a noble
work." An overseer, therefore, must be . . .*
—1 Timothy 3:1-2

As I mentioned a few days ago, I love sports. As a
child, I loved watching all sports, but I loved playing
two in particular. You've already read about my love
for baseball. However, basketball was my true love.
Growing up in the mountains of eastern Kentucky, I
had the same dream of every other boy in the Bluegrass
state: to be in the starting lineup for the University of
Kentucky men's basketball team. I grew up watching
the likes of Kenny Walker, Rex Chapman, and Jamal
Mashburn, and I would think to myself, *Someday, that
will be me. I will be a Kentucky Wildcat.*

I spent countless hours working on my game. Long
after the sun went down, our neighbors could hear the

sound of a basketball bouncing on the pavement in our driveway. I played pick-up games. I played in school leagues. I played in recreational leagues. As I got older, I played for my middle school team, and even for my high school.

However, I never accomplished my dream of starting for the Wildcats. It certainly wasn't because I lacked desire; it was because I lacked the skills necessary to compete at that level. There is a required standard in order to suit up for the University of Kentucky, and I did not meet that standard. I simply was not *qualified* to play college basketball.

You might know of potential candidates who have the desire to be your next pastor. However, having a strong desire to be a pastor isn't enough for someone to actually serve as a pastor. They must meet the required standards. In other words, they must be *qualified*.

During the pastor search, you might be asked to complete a survey regarding the desired characteristics and qualifications you would most like your next pastor to possess. You might prefer someone with a particular skill set. Maybe you would like for him to have at least five years of ministry experience or a certain level of education. Maybe you want him to have a master's degree from one of the seminaries on a particular list. Perhaps you want him to be married with a couple of kids. The list could go on and on.

While there's nothing wrong with having a wish list, there's a danger in allowing your "wish list" to become a "must-have list." The reality is that if the characteristics listed above are your minimum criteria for your next pastor, Jesus Himself would not qualify!

It is interesting that when Paul lays out the biblical qualifications for a pastor, he spends less time on the *externals* than on the *internals*. In other words, a potential pastor's character is much more important than his particular gifts or skills.

Consider the following qualifications Paul lists in 1 Timothy 3:2-7:

> *An overseer, therefore, must be above reproach, the husband of one wife, self-controlled, sensible, respectable, hospitable, able to teach, not an excessive drinker, not a bully but gentle, not quarrelsome, not greedy. He must manage his own household competently and have his children under control with all dignity. (If anyone does not know how to manage his own household, how will he take care of God's church?) He must not be a new convert, or he might become conceited and incur the same condemnation as the devil. Furthermore, he must have a good reputation among outsiders, so that he does not fall into disgrace and the devil's trap.*

During the past few days, we've covered the primary roles of a pastor and have looked at what he is called to do. Notice, though, that the majority of qualifications deal more with who your pastor *is* as a follower of Christ rather than what he is able to *do* for Christ.

Paul writes, *If I speak human or angelic tongues, but do not have love, I am a noisy gong or a clanging cymbal. If I have the gift of prophecy and understand all mysteries and all knowledge, and if I have all faith so that I can move mountains but do not have love, I am nothing* (1 Corinthians 13:1-2). In this passage, Paul emphasizes that doing great works for Christ without the accompanying internal motivations nullifies his service to the Lord, and the same applies to your pastor (and to you, too, for that matter, as we will discuss later).

As your church searches for your next pastor, pray that he will be a man of integrity, a man whose walk matches his talk, and a man who meets the biblical qualifications (albeit imperfectly) – and if he happens to match your wish list as well, that's even better!

Your Role in the Search

- **Review:** Only those who are biblically qualified can serve as pastors.

- **Reflect:** Make a list of qualities you would like your next pastor to possess. Compare your list to those found in 1 Timothy 3:2-7. How do they compare?

- **Renew:** Pray that the Pastor Search Committee will be diligent to examine the biblical qualifications of all pastoral candidates whom they strongly consider.

Week 3 – Be Humble

Most conflicts in churches take place because one or more members selfishly put their own preferences above others. If you are unwilling to humbly defer to the interests and needs of your fellow church members during this season without a pastor, trouble lies ahead. During this week, we'll discuss specific ways of how to commit to an attitude of humility. In doing so, you'll be much more likely to maintain unity within your church during the search.

Day 1

What Your Next Pastor Is Looking for in You

*Make my joy complete by thinking the same
way, having the same love, united in spirit,
intent on one purpose. Do nothing out of
selfish ambition or conceit, but in humility consider others as more important than
yourselves.*
—Philippians 2:2-3

During our last time together, we talked about the
characteristics and qualifications you should look for
in your next pastor, but have you ever thought about it
from the opposite perspective? Have you ever thought
about what your next pastor is looking for in your
church? Has it ever crossed your mind that he might
have a wish list as well? I can promise you he does.

I love the book of Acts. It is riveting to read how the
early church was born and experienced exponential
growth as the gospel was proclaimed in Jerusalem, in

Judea and Samaria, and beyond. In Acts 16, we read that Paul led several people to Christ and that the Philippian church was born. It's an incredible story.

Ten years later, Paul found himself in prison with time on his hands to write a letter to his friends in Philippi. He wrote to encourage them, which he did in several ways throughout the letter. However, in the passage above, he expressed his desire to not only be an encouragement *to* the Philippians, but to be encouraged *by* the Philippians. The way they could do so was by displaying the characteristics on his wish list.

While there is a lot packed into these verses, Paul's wish list can be condensed down to two items: unity and humility. First, Paul wanted the church to be unified, because evidently they were not (see Philippians 4:2-3). Notice how Paul repeatedly used language that indicated his desire for unity: *thinking the **same** way, **same** love, **united** in spirit*, and ***one** purpose* (Philippians 2:2-3, emphasis added).

Unity is also a characteristic that Jesus wanted for the church. In fact, He prayed for it: *I pray not only for these, but also for those who believe in me through their word. **May they all be one**, as you, Father, are in me and I am in you. May they also be in us, so that the world may believe you sent me* (John 17:20-21, emphasis added).

Unfortunately, the church is not always unified. In our sinful natures, it is natural for conflict and division to arise, usually because the second item on Paul's wish list, humility, is missing. As Gavin Ortlund puts it, "Humility is the pathway to unity."[4] When there is

---

4   Gavin Ortlund, *Finding the Right Hills to Die On: The Case for*

no humility among God's people, you will not find unity either.

That's the point Paul makes in Philippians 2:3-4. In verse 3, he encourages the church to *do nothing out of selfish ambition or conceit.* Instead, they should *in humility consider others more important* than themselves. When church members selfishly look out only for their own interests, conflict and division are the guaranteed result, as James 4:1-3 makes clear.

However, Paul offers a better way in verse 4: *Everyone should look not to his own interests, but rather to the interests of others.* This is the way of Jesus, who endured the cross because He was looking out for our interests instead of His own (Philippians 2:5-8).

During a pastor search, this issue of humility is critical. While it is okay to have preferences for your next pastor, it is not okay to turn those preferences into demands. As I've mentioned before, you must avoid allowing your wish list for your next pastor to selfishly become a list of must-haves. If you do so, you have allowed your desires to become demands. When you don't get what you want in the timeframe you want, conflict will soon follow.

So today, make a commitment to be humble throughout this season without a pastor. Commit to putting the needs, interests, and preferences of others above your own. If everyone in your church will make this commitment, the church will remain unified and the Search Committee can go about their work without worrying about division in the church.

Theological Triage (Wheaton, IL: Crossway, 2020), 149.

Unity and humility: that is what Paul was looking for in the Philippian church, and that is exactly what your next pastor will hope to find in your church.

Your Role in the Search

- **Review:** Your next pastor is looking for a church characterized by unity and humility.

- **Reflect:** How would you describe your church right now? Is it characterized more by unity and humility or by pride and division?

- **Respond:** Pray and ask the Lord to help you put the needs and preferences of other church members above your own throughout this interim period.

Day 2

Unrealistic Expectations

"What you're doing is not good," Moses's father-in-law said to him. "You will certainly wear out both yourself and these people who are with you, because the task is too heavy for you. You can't do it alone."
—Exodus 18:17-18

I have led several churches through an exercise I learned from Thom Rainer.[5] During a meeting with a group of church leaders, I will ask them to list all the tasks they expect their pastor to complete during a typical week. Preaching and sermon preparation always make the list. Counseling members and visiting shut-ins are mentioned as well. Outreach and administration are there too. After the list is finished, it's usually quite long.

Next, I will review the list and ask the group to

5   Thom Rainer, "How Many Hours Must a Pastor Work to Satisfy The Congregation?" www.archive.thomrainer.com/2013/07/how-many-hours-must-a-pastor-work-to-satisfy-the-congregation/ (July 24, 2013).

write down how long they expect their pastor to spend in each activity during a typical week. After they have had time to record their answers, I'll return to each item on the list and ask each person to share their response. For example, for sermon preparation, one church leader may expect their pastor to spend fifteen hours per week. Another church leader may expect twenty-five hours per week, and another may expect thirty hours per week. I will record the highest number, and we will move on to the next activity on the list. After repeating these steps for each item on the list, I will calculate the total.

In several years of conducting this exercise with different churches, the total has never been less than one hundred hours per week. Not even once. Keep in mind that this is only among the church leadership. If the exercise was expanded to the whole church, the total would climb even higher.

This exercise proves that regardless of the size of your congregation, it is impossible for your pastor to meet everyone's expectations in your church. Just as Jethro advised Moses, your next pastor simply cannot be expected to do everything. However, that doesn't mean some church members won't place unrealistic expectations on their pastors anyway. Here are four common unrealistic expectations you need to avoid:

Don't expect your next pastor to be Superman. From the exercise above, it's clear that your next pastor will not be Superman, nor should you expect him to be. We will discuss this more later on, but every member of the church has a role to fill. Your pastor can't be responsible for everything, so don't place that burden on him. It's a recipe for disaster.

Don't expect your next pastor to be good at everything. Just as you shouldn't expect your pastor to do everything, you shouldn't expect him to be good at everything either. Everyone is better at some things than others, and that will also be true for your next pastor. Just because he might be a gifted preacher doesn't mean he will be equally skilled at hospital visits. Just because he might be a people person doesn't mean he will be proficient at administrative tasks.

Don't expect your next pastor to be the solution to all of your church's problems. You may have heard the joke that if you find a perfect church, don't join it because it won't be perfect anymore. The truth is there is no perfect church. Every church is made up of sinners. *Forgiven* sinners, but sinners nonetheless. Therefore, every church has problems. Some people mistakenly believe that a new pastor will be the answer to all those problems. However, another old saying is that you can lead a horse to water, but you can't make him drink. While your next pastor may be able to identify some of your church's problems, he can't fix them on his own. Those problems involve people, and those people must be willing to make the necessary adjustments to fix those problems. Placing that burden solely on your next pastor is an unrealistic and unfair expectation.

Don't expect your next pastor to be a church growth expert. Last week, we covered the biblical roles of a pastor. Remember that your pastor is to feed, lead, protect, and comfort the flock (Psalm 23). If he fulfills those four roles, he will be a faithful pastor in the eyes of the Lord. While you can certainly hope that his faithfulness in those four areas will lead your church to numeric growth, you cannot demand it. Your next pastor may fulfill all of these roles, yet the church may not grow at all. This may not have anything to do with your pastor's abilities or efforts, but it could be due to other factors. Perhaps the community around your church is changing. Maybe a large percentage of your church is unengaged in evangelizing the lost. Perhaps your congregation is unwelcoming to guests or unwilling to allow new people to serve.

While it is unfair and unrealistic to place these types of expectations on your pastor, doing so is far too common. Pastors are not meant to serve under this type of pressure. If you insist that he do so, it might not be long before your church is searching for yet another pastor. Therefore, commit to humbly supporting your pastor rather than selfishly demanding him to meet unrealistic expectations.

Your Role in the Search

- **Review:** Avoid placing unrealistic and unfair expectations upon your next pastor.

- **Reflect:** What expectations do you have for your next pastor? Are any of them unrealistic?

- **Respond:** Read Exodus 18:13-27. Make a list of any unrealistic expectations that had been placed upon Moses, either by the people or by Moses himself, and also note how Jethro adjusted those expectations.

Day 3

Disarm the Land Mines

But reject foolish and ignorant disputes,
because you know that they breed quarrels.
The Lord's servant must not quarrel, but
must be gentle to everyone, able to teach,
and patient, instructing his opponents with
gentleness.
—2 Timothy 2:23-25

I've been in ministry long enough now that I am sometimes asked to offer advice to less experienced pastors.
One piece of advice I often share is to *look out for the*
land mines.

As you know, land mines are explosive devices
concealed on or under the ground. When a target
steps on it, the device detonates, mortally wounding
or destroying its victim. Land mines are particularly
dangerous because you don't see them until it's too late.

Every church has land mines as well. They are not

literal land mines, of course, but they are there, and they have the potential to devastate the poor soul who steps on one. Unfortunately, they are also concealed, and a new pastor may not notice it until it is too late. The damage has already been done, and sometimes pastors don't survive.

However, it doesn't have to be that way. Right now, during this season of transition, you and your fellow church members can disarm the land mines in your church so your next pastor doesn't inadvertently injure himself or others.

In order to do so, you must first acknowledge that land mines exist in your church. One land mine might be unwritten rules about certain traditions, ministries, or events in your church that are not to be trifled with. Another might be the order of the worship service. One might be the Easter cantata. Another land mine could be the monthly bake sale to fund summer camp for your students. Whatever they are, they are not to be questioned or challenged. To do so could set off a lethal explosion.

It's not a question of *if* land mines exist in your church; it's only a question of *where* they are. Now is the time for you and your fellow church members to identify their location and take the necessary steps to disarm them. Unfortunately, not every land mine is easily found, so you may need to conduct careful excavation to discover them. Here are a few diagnostic questions to help you identify potential land mines in your church:

What events on the church calendar must never be canceled or changed? Does your church host a large back-to-school bash? Maybe it's a trunk-or-treat event. Perhaps your church has a big fireworks show on Independence Day. Do you have any event that has become so popular or nostalgic that it can never be removed from the calendar without setting off emotional fireworks in your congregation?

Do you have any events or ministries that trump all others? Have you ever tried to add an event to the church calendar only to hear, "Well, you can't do it then because we always have this other event at that time." Or maybe you're told you can't start a new ministry because it could negatively affect the participation in another established ministry. If so, you could step on a land mine if you try to invade its territory.

Are there potential changes that, if introduced by your next pastor, could cost him his job? If the pastor decided to observe the Lord's Supper on a Sunday morning rather than on a Sunday evening, would some church members call for his dismissal? If he replaced the church pews with portable chairs, would he need to pack his bags? If he canceled Sunday night services, would that be a bridge too far? What changes could he potentially make that could spell doom for his ministry at your church?

What preferences held by the majority of your congregation must your next pastor also abide by? Is there a particular Bible version he must preach from? Is there a particular worship style that must not change? Will he be required to ask for prayer requests during the Sunday morning worship service? What traditions are held by your church that must continue?

What hills are you and your fellow church members willing to die on? I'm not talking about the foundational doctrines of the faith. I'm talking about traditions, ministries, and preferences. Which ones do you consider to be non-negotiable?

Questions like these are helpful in identifying potential land mines in your church. Once you identify them, you should have an honest discussion with your fellow church members about them. Perhaps you'll discover that some are not as important as you have made them out to be. However, you might also decide that there are some that *are* non-negotiable for your church. If so, your Pastor Search Committee has an obligation to communicate those to potential candidates. A land mine becomes less dangerous when it loses its element of surprise. If a pastor knows the location of the land mines, he can successfully navigate around them.

However, remember that the goal for your church is to be characterized by humility. Only when you humbly consider these questions will you find that outside of the foundational doctrines of our faith, churches often make mountains out of molehills. Therefore, ask yourself if Jesus would be pleased that you are making such a big deal about this particular ministry, event, or tradition. You might find that this hill is not worth dying on, either for you or for your next pastor.

Your Role in the Search

- **Review:** Identify and remove the land mines in your church before you call your next pastor.

- **Reflect:** Based upon the questions above, what potential land mines are in your church?

- **Respond:** Read 2 Timothy 2:14-26. How many of your church's land mines would Paul describe as *foolish and ignorant disputes*?

Day 4

When the Past Is the Hero

But one thing I do: Forgetting what is
behind and reaching forward to what is
ahead, I pursue as my goal the prize prom-
ised by God's heavenly call in Christ Jesus.
—Philippians 3:13-14

The older I get, the more I understand the nostalgic pull of the good old days. I remember sitting on my grandmother's front porch with my extended family on warm summer evenings. I remember getting lost in the woods with my childhood friends. I remember my mom cooking a grilled cheese sandwich for me every day. I miss those days. Whenever I take a trip down memory lane, there's always a part of me that wants to stay there awhile.

If you've been a member of your church for several years, I'm sure you have fond memories as well. There are probably times when you find yourself desiring to go back there too – dinner on the grounds; packed Sunday school classrooms; weeklong revivals – such happy memories.

Trust me, I understand. The good old days are the good old days for a reason. Unfortunately, some churches try to stay in the good old days. In doing so, they reveal that the past is their hero. These churches talk about the past frequently and are unwilling to make changes that could be interpreted in any way as dishonoring the past. "That's the way we've always done it" is a common phrase.

While it's fine to honor the past, your church can't live there. Doing so will make present and future ministry quite difficult for your next pastor and other church leaders.

In the passage above, Paul encourages his Philippian brothers and sisters to follow his example to forget what lies behind and focus on what lies ahead. As you prepare for your next pastor, here are several suggestions for applying this passage:

Remember that a beloved former pastor is not your pastor anymore. I understand; I have fond memories of some former pastors as well. For a season, they fed, led, protected, and comforted my soul. I am grateful for the various ways they impacted my life. But that season has come to an end. Therefore, don't pick up the phone or text a former pastor every time you need spiritual guidance. He isn't your pastor anymore; allow your new pastor to be your pastor.

Avoid comparisons between former pastors and your new pastor. Try not to say, "That's not the way our former pastor did it." Just as you probably wouldn't enjoy hearing about all the great things from his previous church, he probably would prefer not to hear about how he will have a hard time filling a beloved former pastor's shoes. Allow him the freedom to pastor your church the way God leads him to do so.

Avoid comparisons between former pastors' wives and your new pastor's wife. For all of the same reasons listed above, your new pastor's wife does not need to constantly hear about how her predecessor did things. As we will discuss in future topics, she already has enough on her plate without trying to live up to someone else's reputation.

Avoid posting historical artifacts in prominent places. Again, while it is appropriate to honor the past, your new pastor will probably not want to see a huge oil painting of a former pastor with a thirty-year tenure hanging in the church foyer. It will cast too long of a shadow. A church library or historical room is an appropriate place to collect and display artifacts from the church's past. Just don't do so in ways that imply that the church's past may be more important than its future.

Learn from the past. The good old days might not be as good as we remember. We tend to recall the good times, while the tough times are more likely to fade from our memories. However, as the old saying goes, those who forget the past are doomed to repeat it. Consider how many times Israel forgot about their past mistakes and how that led to devastating consequences. Therefore, don't forget past lessons learned, for they can help you and your church make better decisions in the future.

Talk about the future. While it is fun to take a trip down memory lane, it is also exciting to dream about the future. Talk to your fellow church members about your hopes, dreams, and fears regarding the church's future. The more you talk about the future of your church, the more you will invest in it.

I have a ton of great memories from my past. I'm sure you do too. But if you commit to being humble, you will not selfishly allow the church's past to dictate its future. The past cannot be the hero of your church. That spot has already been claimed by Jesus.

Your Role in the Search

- **Review:** Honor the past, but don't live there.
- **Reflect:** Is the past the hero in your church? How can you tell?
- **Respond:** Read Philippians 3. Pray and ask the Lord to help you imitate Paul's attitude toward his past, as well as toward his future.

Day 5

Deny Yourself

If anyone wants to follow after me, let him deny himself, take up his cross daily, and follow me.
—Luke 9:23

As a parent of two boys, I have found myself teaching my sons many lessons over the years. I've taught them how to ride a bike, how to shoot a basketball, how to tie their shoes, and how to open doors for others. One thing I did not need to teach them was how to be selfish. They figured that one out on their own. In fact, one of the first words that either of them said was "Mine!"

I'm guessing that your kids or grandkids didn't have to learn how to be selfish either. From a young age, our sin nature shows itself in our unwillingness to share. Therefore, it is unnecessary to teach others how to be selfish; it comes standard with every toddler.

Unfortunately, selfishness doesn't always fade away as a child grows and matures. The reality is that we struggle with selfishness and pride throughout our lives. We want things *our* way, and we are willing to fight to make sure we get our way. As we've seen in recent days, this is not just true outside the church. Those inside the church can also be selfish.

However, as Jesus makes clear in Luke 9:23, it's hard to hold on to your selfishness and follow Jesus at the same time. In fact, it's impossible. You must be willing to deny yourself on a daily basis. During this season without a pastor, you need to deny yourself in at least three ways.

First, you must be willing to put the needs of others above your own. As your church makes decisions now and in the future – when your new pastor arrives – don't immediately ask how those decisions affect you. That's an attitude of selfishness. Instead, ask questions about how the decision or change will affect others. *Is this decision or change best for the church? Is it best for the community? Is it best for the lost?* If the answer to any of those questions is yes, how it affects you personally becomes irrelevant. That's how you know you're putting the needs of others above your own.

Second, don't allow your desires to become demands. As I've mentioned previously, everyone has preferences. Everyone prefers things to work out a certain way. The problem is when we allow those preferences or desires to become demands. At that moment, we have concluded in our heart that we cannot be happy unless our demand is met. If that occurs, our demand has become an idol in our heart. Therefore, be careful about making selfish demands of your Pastor Search Committee, your new pastor and his family, or even your fellow church members. Doing so reveals that you are not denying yourself.

Third, make every effort to follow Jesus. If you read Luke 9:23, you'll see that Jesus explains that our denial of self has a purpose: it paves the way to follow Jesus. Once you are no longer worried about yourself, you'll find it easier to spend time with Him. You'll find it easier to imitate Him. You'll find it easier to obey Him. You'll find yourself becoming more and more like Him every day, and that's the ultimate goal of every believer.

Denying yourself is difficult. In fact, making the commitment to be humble is the most difficult of the five commitments for the church during the search. However, if you and your fellow church members can make this commitment, you have the potential to transform your church in ways you can't imagine.

Your Role in the Search

- **Review:** If you are going to commit to being humble during the search, you must deny your selfish preferences.

- **Reflect:** How have you struggled with denying yourself during the past week?

- **Respond:** Read Matthew 10. In what specific ways would the disciples have to deny themselves in order to accomplish the mission Jesus gave them?

Week 4 – Be Prayerful

Prayer is essential for the church during the search. Following the example of the Lord Himself, you and your fellow church members must bathe every part of the search process in prayer. Therefore, you'll be challenged this week to commit to frequent and fervent times of prayer, both individually and corporately. You'll also learn several practical ways to pray for your church, your Pastor Search Committee, your next pastor, and your next pastor's family.

The Forgotten Power of Prayer

The prayer of a righteous person is very powerful in its effect.
—James 5:16

During your search for a pastor, there will probably be times when the church is called to prayer at significant moments during the process. Perhaps the Search Committee is having difficulty deciding between a small number of good candidates. Perhaps they have extended an invitation to a candidate and the church is awaiting his response. Maybe the church is experiencing conflict as the search continues, and the call to prayer is simply to restore the church's unity. The possibilities are endless, but know this: the church should devote much time to prayer during the search process.

If you do so, you'll follow the example of Jesus. We read in Luke 5:16 that while the news about Jesus continued to spread, and as large crowds gathered around Him, He would often slip away to the wilderness to pray. Over and over again, we read how Jesus made prayer a priority. The time of day didn't matter; Jesus' disciples often found Him praying. He prayed early in the morning (Mark 1:35), in the middle of the day (Matthew 14:22-23), and sometimes all night long (Luke 6:12). While He often prayed alone, there were times when He prayed with others (Luke 9:28). Not only did He pray *with* others, but He prayed *for* others (Luke 22:31-32). Truly, Jesus made prayer a priority.

Unfortunately, while prayer was a priority for Jesus, it was often a problem for His disciples. In Matthew 26:36-46, we read about Jesus praying in the garden of Gethsemane immediately before His arrest. He had taken Peter, James, and John along with Him, asking them to watch and pray as well. Unfortunately, while Jesus was only a short distance away praying, His disciples were napping. After waking them up, Jesus went away to pray a second time. Again, His disciples fell asleep. Upon discovering them sleeping once again, Jesus didn't even bother to wake them up. He went away and prayed alone for the third time. Indeed, prayer was a problem for the disciples.

The reality is that prayer continues to be a problem for many Christians. Prayer is something we know we *should do*, but often don't take the time to *actually do*. While research reveals that prayer is *the* best practice during a pastor search,[6] those who consult churches

---

6   Jason Lowe, "Searching For Ways to Search For A Pastor: An Examination of the Best & Worst Practices in the Pastor Search Process," www.jasonalowe.com/wp-content/uploads/2018/06/pastor-search-survey-results-report.pdf (June 4, 2018).

during this season of transition identified a lack of prayer as one of the biggest mistakes made during the process.

If church members like yourself will make the commitment to be prayer warriors throughout the search process, it could make this time in your church's history one of the greatest displays of God's power that you ever experience as a congregation.

Prayer was certainly a powerful weapon for the first-century church. In Acts 4, we read about how two of these disciples (Peter and John) were arrested and warned not to speak or teach in the name of Jesus anymore. After their release, they went and told the church all that happened, and the church prayed: *And now, Lord, consider their threats, and grant that your servants may speak your word with all boldness, while you stretch out your hand for healing, and signs and wonders are performed through the name of your holy servant Jesus* (Acts 4:29-30). Then we read, *When they had prayed, the place where they were assembled was shaken, and they were all filled with the Holy Spirit and began to speak the word of God boldly* (Acts 4:31).

Think back to the occasion when Jesus prayed all night long. Notice that He had a specific reason for doing so: *During those days he went out to the mountain to pray and spent all night in prayer to God. When daylight came, he summoned his disciples, and he chose twelve of them, whom he also named apostles* (Luke 6:12-13).

Pause and think about that for a moment. Before Jesus selected His twelve disciples, He spent an entire night praying about His selection. This is simply amazing! If the Lord of the universe found it necessary to pray *all night long* before selecting those who would lead His church, how much more do you need to do so?

Just as prayer was a powerful weapon for the early church, it can also be a powerful weapon for your church – but you must commit to making it a priority during this interim season.

There are many specific ways you can pray throughout your church's search for a pastor. Over the next few days, I will suggest several of these ways. Before we do so, though, make the commitment today to be a prayer warrior so you can witness the awesome power of God on full display in the days, weeks, and months ahead!

Your Role in the Search

- **Review:** Prayer is an essential weapon for the church during the search.

- **Reflect:** How is your personal prayer life right now? How many times have you prayed for the Pastor Search Process?

- **Respond:** Skim through the book of Acts and take special note of the early church's dependency on prayer.

Day 2

Pray for Your Church

I give thanks to my God for every remem-
brance of you, always praying with joy for
all of you in my every prayer.
—Philippians 1:3-4

There are few things more assuring in life than to
know someone is fervently and consistently praying for you. Just this morning, I received a text from a
friend who told me he had prayed for me – and that's
not the first time he has done so. He has sent me many
similar texts in the past.

I don't know about you, but that's a great way to
start the day! It is encouraging to know that someone
took the time to go to the God of the universe on my
behalf, to intercede for me, and to cry out to the One who
has all power and authority. After receiving a text like
that, I feel as if I could charge hell with a water pistol!

As you begin to think about specific ways to pray

during the search, there are several intentional ways to do so. We begin today by discussing ways you can pray for your fellow church members. As you consider these specific prayer recommendations, be encouraged that you are being prayed for by your brothers and sisters in similar ways.

Pray for humility. Remember – if there's no humility, there's no unity. Pray that your church will follow Jesus' example by putting the needs and interests of others above their own. Pray that your church will not demand that your next pastor fit a certain profile that Jesus Himself could not even fit.

Pray for patience. It's been mentioned several times already that the average Pastor Search Process takes twelve to eighteen months. However, in an on-demand culture, it's hard to wait for anything. Therefore, it is likely that you or your fellow church members will grow impatient at times, and that could lead to unwarranted criticism of the Search Committee. Pray that your church will remain patient so the committee can conduct their work free from the distraction of constant pressure from the congregation.

Pray for commitment. When a pastor vacancy occurs, church members often slack off in their commitments to the church. Pray that doesn't happen in your congregation. Although you might be without a pastor right now, the head of the church is still present (Colossians 1:18), and He is worthy of your continued commitment to worship and service. In addition, your fellow church members are counting on you!

Pray for productivity. Church members who remain committed during an interim period are much more likely to continue to bear spiritual fruit. Opportunities for ministry abound whether you have a pastor or not. There are still church members who need encouragement. There are still Sunday school classes that need to be taught. There are still lost people in your community who need to be reached. There are still babies in the nursery who need to be cared for. Pray that your church continues to bear fruit during this season.

Pray for evangelistic faithfulness. Many church members are tempted to leave the church's evangelistic efforts to the pastor. While this is unhelpful and unbiblical, the reality is that this mindset leads to few evangelistic efforts when the church doesn't have a pastor. If the pastor is not there to do it, it doesn't happen. Pray that you and your fellow members recognize that the Great Commission mandate applies to all church members, not just to the pastor and church leaders. Pray that your church will actually increase its evangelistic efforts during the interim period.

Pray for protection. Just as Paul warned the Ephesian elders that savage wolves would attack the church after his departure (Acts 20:29-31), Satan will try to attack your church while you are without a pastor (1 Peter 5:8).

Pray for the Lord's protection as you seek the next shepherd for your flock.

There are many other ways you can pray for your church during the search, but this list is meant to give you a few ideas. Your church is in a critical moment in its history, and this entire season needs to be bathed in prayer. Therefore, I would encourage you to add these prayer suggestions to your daily prayer list.

If you and your fellow church members will commit to praying daily for each other in these ways, you will be encouraged and your church will be strengthened.

Your Role in the Search

- **Review:** Daily prayer for your church is crucial during the search.

- **Reflect:** How have you been praying for your church during the interim period?

- **Respond:** Read Philippians 1:3-11, and take special note of the different ways Paul prayed for the Philippian church.

Day 3

Pray for Your Pastor Search Committee

*While Moses held up his hand, Israel pre-
vailed, but whenever he put his hand down,
Amalek prevailed. When Moses's hands grew
heavy, they took a stone and put it under him,
and he sat down on it. Then Aaron and Hur
supported his hands, one on one side and one
on the other so that his hands remained steady
until the sun went down. So Joshua defeated
Amalek and his army with the sword.*
—Exodus 17:11-13

One of the first actions your church will need to take
during the Pastor Search Process is to form a Pastor
Search Committee. Your church's Constitution and
Bylaws may provide direction as to how the committee should be formed. These documents may specify
the number of members for the committee or specific
positions (such as the deacon chairman or the Sunday

school director) who will automatically be appointed to the committee.

Regardless of the specific parameters, churches are often tempted to rush this process so the committee can get to work as soon as possible. However, rushing through this step could produce devastating consequences down the road. Therefore, your church desperately needs the right people to serve on the committee. That's why it is critical for you and your church to spend a significant amount of time in prayer *before* selecting the members of your Pastor Search Committee. Here are a few ways to pray before you form the committee:

Pray that the church will select members who do not have a personal agenda. Committee members with agendas usually don't have the best interest of the church at heart. They may put their own interests above the interests of others, which can make the search process more difficult. Pray that your Search Committee members will not pursue selfish interests.

Pray that the church will select members who will be committed to the search process. I don't know everything about your church, but I know that many of your church members lead busy lives. When forming a Pastor Search Committee, there's an understandable tendency to fill it with members who are regularly active in the church. While that's certainly better than the alternative of selecting committee members who are mostly inactive, you need to pray that your committee members will have enough time to devote to the search process.

Pray that the church will select members who are spiritually mature. When King Solomon died, his son Rehoboam reigned in his place. However, when faced with his first test of leadership, Rehoboam showed that he was not mature enough for the task. Instead of listening to the counsel of the older men who had wisely counseled his father, he followed the foolish advice of his young friends – with disastrous consequences (1 Kings 12:1-24). Similarly, the biggest mistake churches can make is to place someone on the Search Committee who is not spiritually mature enough for the task. It could lead to disastrous consequences as well.

Once your Pastor Search Committee has been formed, they will desperately need your prayer support throughout the process. Much like Aaron and Hur held up Moses' hands so Israel could defeat Amalek (Exodus 17:11-13), your Search Committee needs you to lift them up in prayer so they will be successful in their work. Here are several ways you can pray for the Search Committee once they begin their work:

Pray that the committee will be unified. Just as your church needs to be unified, you need to pray that your Search Committee will be unified. Pray that they will be unified in their goals, their guidelines, and their commitment. When the time comes, pray that they will be unified in their selection of the man they feel God is calling to be your next pastor. Much of the pastor search will be a subjective process, so unity is critical.

Pray that the committee will be prayerful. It may seem odd to pray for someone else to be prayerful. But your Search Committee has a huge task ahead of them. They will meet on a regular basis during the coming months, and they will be tempted to neglect prayer because other items on their task list will demand their time and attention. Pray that the committee will bathe every decision in prayer.

Pray that the committee will be patient. The church needs to be patient with the Search Committee, and the Search Committee needs to be patient with the search *process.* The committee will constantly feel the pressure (whether spoken or unspoken) from the church, and they will be tempted to rush the process at times. Pray that they resist that temptation.

Pray that the committee will practice godly wisdom and discernment. Reviewing stacks of résumés, conducting numerous interviews, and trying to decide between two qualified candidates all require wisdom and discernment. Pray that the committee will make wise decisions throughout the process.

Pray that the committee will be thorough. The best search committees do their homework throughout the process. Pray that your committee will be thorough in their study of your church's culture and needs, as well as in their examination of pastoral candidates.

Pastor Search Committees bear a tremendous responsibility, and they need your prayer support. Commit to lifting them up on a daily basis.

Your Role in the Search

- **Review:** Your Pastor Search Committee desperately needs your prayer support.

- **Reflect:** How often have you prayed for your Pastor Search Committee thus far?

- **Respond:** What other ways can you pray for your Pastor Search Committee? Write them down in a prayer journal and consider sharing them with your fellow church members.

Day 4

Pray for Your Next Pastor

*God is my witness, whom I serve with my
spirit in telling the good news about his Son
– that I constantly mention you, always
asking in my prayers that if it is somehow
in God's will, I may now at last succeed in
coming to you.*
—Romans 1:9-10

When Paul first penned the words of Romans 1:9-10, he had not yet been to Rome. He had never met the believers in the church there. However, it was not due to a lack of desire, as he explained a few verses later: *Now I don't want you to be unaware, brothers and sisters, that I often planned to come to you (but was prevented until now) in order that I might have a fruitful ministry among you* (Romans 1:13). Although Paul had never met this body of believers, he prayed for them, and he regularly asked the Lord to allow him to meet them face-to-face.

Right now, you don't know the identity of your next pastor. It's likely you've never met him. Even though that might be the case, you can follow Paul's example and pray for him even before you know his name. Consider these ways to pray for your next pastor right now:

Pray that God will give him the strength to leave his current ministry. If your next pastor is currently serving in another ministry role, that ministry will have to come to an end before his ministry at your church can begin. That means he will have to say many goodbyes. If he has been in his current role for several years, he will probably be leaving many close friends. This won't be easy. Pray that the Lord will give him the strength to do so.

Pray that God will give him a love for your church. If the Lord is calling him to your church, your next pastor should begin to feel drawn to the people of your congregation. Pray that the Lord would give him a deep love and concern for the members of your flock, especially if circumstances in his current ministry situation have made it harder for him to love others. Pray that he will not allow any past negative experiences to influence the way he cares for your church.

Pray that God will give him a burden for the lost in your community. Not only should your next pastor have a deep love for those inside the flock of your church, but he should also have a burden for those in your community who have yet to profess faith in Jesus Christ. Pray that he will be overwhelmed by the spiritual lostness in your local community and will lead the church to take specific steps to penetrate the darkness. Pray also that your church will not place the entire burden of reaching the lost on your pastor. Be willing to join him in the work of proclaiming the gospel to a lost and dying world.

Pray that God will give him a strong desire to teach and preach the whole counsel of God. As we have seen in previous readings, pastors have a lot on their plate. Because of the demands on their time, they might not devote as much time to sermon preparation as they would like. Pray that the Lord will help your next pastor to make this his highest priority so that he can regularly feed your church a steady and spiritually nutritious diet of God's Word.

Pray that he will make significant time for his family. You will probably be excited when your new pastor arrives. He will probably be excited too. However, he may be so eager to get off to a good start in his new ministry setting that he neglects his responsibilities as a husband and a father (if applicable). Remember – your pastor's first ministry is to his family (1 Timothy 3:4), so pray that he does not neglect those he loves the most.

Pray that he will be faithful to fulfill the biblical roles of a shepherd. Pray that he devotes the majority of his time to the four primary roles of a shepherd. Pray that he will feed, lead, protect, and comfort the flock in a way that honors the Lord and builds up His church.

There are many other ways you can pray for your next pastor, but these are intended to get you started. As you think about other ways to pray for him, share your ideas with your fellow church members. Spend time together on a regular basis crying out to the Lord on behalf of your next pastor.

Your Role in the Search

- **Review:** You can follow Paul's example by praying for your next pastor now, before you ever meet him face-to-face.

- **Reflect:** What other ways can you pray for your next pastor? Write them down in a prayer journal and consider sharing them with your fellow church members.

- **Respond:** Consider a day of prayer and fasting for your church in order to devote a full day to praying for your next pastor.

Pray for Your Next Pastor's Family

*Husbands, love your wives, just as Christ
loved the church and gave himself for her. .
. . Fathers, don't stir up anger in your children, but bring them up in the training and
instruction of the Lord.*
—Ephesians 5:25; 6:4

'll never forget when I walked through the empty
parsonage with our two young sons for the first time.
My wife and I were confident God was calling us to
this new ministry assignment. We had prayed about
it for months. We had completed multiple interviews.
We had already received a unanimous vote by the
Association's executive board. We had even walked
through the parsonage before. But this was the first
time our two sons had learned anything about what
was about to happen. They were both preschoolers at

the time, so there had not been any need to share the news with them.

However, I'll never forget the tears that streamed down our four-year-old's little cheeks when he realized this was going to be his new home. He was devastated. He didn't want to leave his friends. He didn't want to give up his big bedroom for the smaller one in the new house. He didn't want to give up his big yard. His young mind could not understand why we had to move.

As a parent, you never want to see your child in pain, whether physical or emotional, yet there was little I could do to comfort my son in that moment; from his perspective, I was the source of his pain.

Whenever you call your next pastor, there's a good chance he won't join your church by himself. If he's married, he will be accompanied by his wife and any children still living at home. I can assure you that my family's experience is not unique. Even though it will be clear that God is leading his family to make the move, it will still be difficult. Therefore, while it is important to pray for your next pastor before you meet him, it is equally important to pray for his family. Here are several practical ways to pray for those who will come along with your next pastor:

Pray that your pastor's wife will develop new friendships quickly. While your next pastor will begin to develop new relationships and friendships almost immediately, that may not be the case for his wife, especially if she has young children at home. Her interaction with her new church family will probably be more limited.

Therefore, pray that the Lord will use some of the ladies in your church to befriend your pastor's wife and show her that she, too, is a part of the family.

Pray that your pastor's wife will adjust to the community. While your next pastor will be busy meeting his new church members, his wife will be left with the responsibility of getting established at new medical and dental offices, securing needed utilities for the home, enrolling the children in school, and finding the closest grocery store. Pray that she is able to do so with minimal setbacks or frustrations. Pray also that your church will go above and beyond in supporting her with these tasks.

Pray that your pastor's wife will not be subjected to unrealistic expectations. You will be searching for the man God is calling to shepherd the flock at your church. You are not calling his wife to the same task. Her primary ministry is to love and support her husband so he can fulfill his calling to shepherd your church. Your next pastor should have a written job description. His wife should not, unless you have hired her for a separate paid position! Therefore, pray that your church doesn't place unrealistic expectations on her. Allow her to serve her husband first, and then to serve in the church however God leads, just like you.

Pray that your pastor's children will also adjust to their new church family and community. It's hard to be a pastor's kid. Whether they like it or not, the pastor and his family live under a microscope. This reality can place an incredible amount of pressure on a child. Add this ongoing pressure to the stress of a new church, a new school, and a new community, and it can almost be too much for some children to bear. Pray that the Lord will help your next pastor's children make new friendships. Pray that they will not be placed under any unnecessary or unrealistic expectations from your church. Pray that your church lets them be kids while they are kids.

You will formally vote to call a new pastor. In reality, God is calling a new family. Pray that all are able to make the necessary adjustments as quickly as possible.

Your Role in the Search

- **Review:** Your next pastor's wife and children need your prayers just as much as your next pastor does.

- **Reflect:** Have you ever considered the emotional toll a new ministry assignment can have on your pastor's family?

- **Respond:** Make a list of practical ways you can help your next pastor's wife and children adjust to their new church and community.

Week 5 - Be Patient

One of the biggest mistakes Pastor Search Committees make is rushing the search process. This often happens because the committee feels the pressure of anxious church members who pepper them with questions or complaints about the length of the process. Given the fact that the average search process takes twelve to eighteen months, you must commit to be patient and allow the Search Committee to do their work, free from ongoing congregational pressure. During this week, you'll learn the five phases of the Pastor Search Process and why your patience is vital to a positive outcome.

Day 1

The Need for Patience

Therefore, brothers and sisters, be patient
until the Lord's coming. See how the farmer
waits for the precious fruit of the earth and is
patient until it receives the early and the late
rains. You also must be patient.
—James 5:7-8

I once had a conversation with a dear brother in Christ who told me that he refused to pray for patience. When I asked him why, he responded, "Because God might give it to me!" After having a good laugh together, he explained that the only way he would learn how to be patient was by waiting on something, and he didn't want to do so. Even after I reminded him that Paul lists patience as a fruit of the Spirit (Galatians 5:22), he still wasn't convinced.

Perhaps you're like my friend. Maybe you don't like to wait either. If so, you're not alone. Many of our meals come from fast-food restaurants. Most of our entertainment comes from on-demand streaming services. We no longer wait for the evening news because we can access the news anytime we want with a simple swipe of our finger. I think it is safe to say that most of us don't like to be patient. We want things done yesterday.

If that describes you, this season in between pastors might be difficult for you. The Pastor Search Process is not usually a quick process. As has been mentioned several times already, the average Pastor Search Process for most churches (regardless of size) takes between twelve and eighteen months – so you might want to start praying for patience. On the bright side, though, at least that is something you don't have to wait for. You can start praying right now!

The Greek word for *patience* used in Galatians 5:22 is the word *makrothumia*, and it literally means "long suffering." It is often used in the context of our relationships with other people. It means that even when you are provoked by others, you don't lose your temper. With that understanding, the best way for the church to practice patience during the search is to remember how patient God has been with us.

When Adam and Eve ate the fruit from the forbidden tree (Genesis 3:6), God could have killed them immediately. When Cain murdered Abel (Genesis 4:8), God could have ended it all there. When He brought the flood (Genesis 6:7-8), He could have let Noah and his family and all the animals die along with the rest of the world. When the people of Israel made the golden calf (Exodus 32), God could have brought fire down from heaven and consumed them. When David sinned with Bathsheba and had Uriah killed (2 Samuel 11), God could have taken away his throne and ended his life. When you and I sin against God and display the works of the flesh, God would be justified in ending our lives immediately.

But He doesn't do that.

Why? Because over and over and over again, the Bible says, *The Lord is compassionate and gracious, slow to anger and abounding in faithful love* (Psalm 103:8; also see Exodus 34:6; Numbers 14:18; 1 Peter 3:20; Nehemiah 9:17; Psalm 86:15; Jonah 4:2; and Joel 2:13 for a small sampling). In other words, God is patient with us!

Because God continues to be so patient with us, He expects us to be patient with one another. In James 5:9, we see how this applies to the life of a believer: *Do not complain about one another.* In other words, don't fight with one another. Don't grumble about one another. Don't participate in gossip or slander. In the context of your Pastor Search Committee, it means you don't get upset if the committee doesn't present a new pastor candidate in your preferred timeframe.

Instead of complaining about the Search Committee, why not spend time thanking the Lord for their sacrifice and dedication to serve in such a difficult role? Don't just thank the Lord privately in prayer, but encourage your Search Committee members by personally thanking them. Tell them you're praying for them. Tell them you support them. Tell them it's okay to take their time. Instead of grumbling against them, encourage them.

Doing so probably won't speed up the process (I know – I wish it would, too!), but it will help you and your church produce the spiritual fruit of patience. In the grand scheme of things, being conformed to the image of Christ is infinitely more important than securing a new pastor in record time anyway (see Romans 8:29).

Your Role in the Search

- **Review:** You must exercise patience during the Pastor Search Process.

- **Reflect:** Think about a time when you had difficulty waiting for something. What were the reasons why it was hard to wait?

- **Respond:** As difficult as it may be, ask the Lord to use this time to produce the spiritual fruit of patience in your life and in the lives of your fellow church members.

Day 2

The Setup Phase

*God patiently waited in the days of Noah
while the ark was being prepared.*
—1 Peter 3:20

One reason why church members grow impatient during a pastor search is because they don't understand the process. They don't know about all the steps involved. They don't know about the potential setbacks. They don't fully understand how long it takes to review résumés and to conduct interviews. All they know is that the Pastor Search Process is taking longer than they would like. So they grow impatient.

Because you're reading this book, you know this doesn't have to be the case with you. While every Pastor Search Process is unique, there are general phases that every Pastor Search Process will follow. During the course of this week, I will cover these phases in greater detail. My hope in doing so is that as you begin to have a greater understanding of the process, you will be more likely to be patient with those who have been given the responsibility to find your next pastor.

Even though God had already revealed His plan to destroy all flesh by the flood, the verse above tells us that God waited patiently for one specific reason: the ark was still being prepared. Biblical scholars disagree on how long it took Noah to build the ark, but even the shortest estimates say it was between twenty and forty years. During that time, God waited. Although He had a plan, several preparations were necessary in order to carry out the plan.

The goal of your Pastor Search Process is to find your next pastor. That's the plan. But before your church can do so, there has to be a time of preparation. Those preparation steps take place during the first phase of the Pastor Search Process – known as the Setup Phase. During this phase, several activities will take place.

First, your church leaders will need to determine who is responsible for securing ongoing pulpit supply for your church. Discussions will also take place regarding the feasibility of calling an interim pastor to assist during this season of transition.

Second, your leaders will refer to your church's Constitution and Bylaws for direction regarding the election of your Pastor Search Committee. Once the committee is in place, they will begin to meet and get organized, which will include the election of several officers (such as chairman, vice-chairman, and secretary).

They may also receive training during this time from a denominational representative who has experience in helping churches during the search.

Next, your Search Committee will begin to establish a few ground rules for how decisions will be made. For example, they might decide that all decisions have to be unanimous, or they might decide that two-thirds majority is sufficient. They will also need to develop a communication strategy for how they will share updates with your church. They will have to agree on confidentiality guidelines. They might even consider drafting a Search Committee member covenant that they each sign.

Finally, your Search Committee and church leaders might work together to decide what they want to do to help the congregation prepare for the search process. That could include a Search Committee commissioning service during which the church prays over the Search Committee members as they begin their work. It could include a season of prayer and fasting. It might include providing copies of this book for your church members to read together. It might include providing other books or resources for your church. It could include inviting a denominational representative to speak to your church to help them know what to expect during the coming months. The possibilities are endless.

You might not notice many of the actions taken during the Setup Phase, but you can be confident these things are necessary. Because the number of tasks is large, it's not uncommon for this first phase to take at least two or three months.

Think about that. There may be folks in your church who think the whole process should be completed in three months – that the committee should be ready to present a new candidate by that time. However, the reality is that most churches will still be getting ready to conduct the search after three months. Since that is the case, you need to exercise patience. Just as God waited patiently while the ark was being prepared, so you need to be patient while the search process is being prepared.

Your Role in the Search

- **Review:** There are many steps that need to be completed before the Pastor Search Committee can begin to search for a new pastor.

- **Reflect:** Describe your understanding of the Pastor Search Process prior to today's reading.

- **Respond:** Read Genesis 6:1-7:10. Record your observations in a journal about God's patience as Noah built the ark.

Day 3

The Study Phase

For which of you, wanting to build a tower,
doesn't first sit down and calculate the cost
to see if he has enough to complete it?
—Luke 14:28

'm not a fan of the car-buying experience. I don't like the scripted questions from the salesmen, such as, "So, what's it going to take to get you in this car today?" I don't like high-pressure sales tactics. I don't like when the dealer tries to lowball me on my trade-in. I don't like it when the person I'm negotiating with is not the person sitting across the desk from me. Can I get an amen? (My apologies if you are a car salesman!)

Given my distaste for the experience, I will not step onto the lot until I have already done my homework. I will conduct online research for weeks, comparing prices and models and figuring out how far I will have to travel to test drive the vehicle. Since I have a degree in statistics, I will use my little spreadsheets to slice and dice the data until I'm confident I have found a good deal.

Unfortunately, my current approach to car buying hasn't always been my approach. I once made an impulse buy on a car without doing my homework, and I made a terrible deal. I refuse to make that same mistake again. I always do my homework now.

In the verse above (Luke 14:28), Jesus asks a rhetorical question to the great crowds who were following Him. In essence, He taught that becoming His disciple would be costly. They needed to take the time to count the cost before following Him. But there's also a more subtle point to this verse. The rhetorical nature of His question reveals that according to Jesus, common sense should tell you that major decisions require adequate time to thoroughly study the situation. This applies to buying a car as well as to calling a pastor.

Before they rush into the actual search, Search Committees need to take the time to study the situation in order to conduct an informed search. They need to do their homework. That's why the second phase of the Pastor Search Process is the Study Phase. In this phase, many activities will be taking place. Just like the Setup Phase, you'll know about a few of them, but not all.

First, your Pastor Search Committee will want to have an idea of the specific characteristics you need in your next pastor before they start looking. In order to assist in this process, they may complete an assessment to help them identify the values that are most important to your church. They may or may not ask you and your fellow church members to complete this assessment. Regardless of whether you complete one or not, the results can help the committee identify pastor candidates who have similar values as your church. This will help them find a man who is a good fit. For example, perhaps your church is passionate about missions. If so, your Search Committee might want to look for a candidate who shares that passion.

Similarly, the committee may seek to identify your church's current strengths and challenges by surveying the congregation. This will assist them in searching for candidates who may have strengths in areas where the church is not as strong and needs to grow.

Next, the committee will need to spend time reviewing and revising your pastor's job description (or writing one if no job description exists). They will also need to develop a fair compensation package, using available resources to discover comparable pay packages from churches that are of similar size and have a similar budget.

Finally, your committee will need to develop a church and community profile to be shared with your top candidates. This profile will help interested candidates pray about God's will concerning your church. This profile may include a copy of the Constitution and Bylaws, a written history of the church, a copy of the church budget, a pictorial directory, copies of recent worship bulletins or newsletters, recent census statistics, information about local schools, maps of the community, and other similar items.

Pastor Search Committees have a lot of work to complete before diving into the actual search. Therefore, the Study Phase takes time. Just like the Setup Phase, it's not uncommon for this phase to take several months. As Jesus implied in Luke 14, though, taking the time to study the situation before making any major decision is good common sense.

If you're keeping track, it's quite possible that the first two phases could take as long as a combined six months, without the actual search even yet beginning! That is why it is imperative that you and your fellow church members remain patient.

The Pastor Search Process is a marathon, not a sprint. So take a deep breath and be prepared to wait on the Lord as He works through your Search Committee.

Your Role in the Search

- **Review:** Your Pastor Search Committee must take time to do their homework in order to find a pastor who will be a good fit for your church.

- **Reflect:** What are the reasons why it is important to study, even if you don't enjoy doing so?

- **Respond:** Spend time today in deep study of a biblical passage of your choosing. Record your observations about the experience.

Day 4

The Search Phase

Ask, and it will be given to you. Seek, and you will find. Knock, and the door will be opened to you.
—Matthew 7:7

If you've ever driven through the Appalachian Mountains, you've probably noticed two character- istics of the roads: they are seldom straight, and they are seldom level. Although the transportation system has certainly improved, it still takes a long time to travel what appears to be a short distance on a map. Ten miles might take twenty minutes or more, especially if you're crossing a mountain during the trip.

The Search Phase is a lot like driving through the mountains. The road is seldom straight, and it is seldom level. Your Search Committee will encounter sharp turns they didn't see coming. They will need to navigate around potholes and bumps in the road. Sometimes they might burn a lot of fuel to move forward just a few feet. While the previous phases are straightforward, the Search Phase is often the longest part of the journey, and it's also the most unpredictable. As your Search Committee enters this phase, several decisions will need to be made.

First, they will need to determine the scope of the search. Will it be a national, statewide, or local search? The answer to this question will have a great impact on the number of résumés the committee is likely to receive. A local search will produce less résumés, while a national search could produce hundreds of résumés. This is a decision the committee cannot take lightly, and they will need to consider many factors before making it.

The Search Committee will also need to determine how they will receive résumés. It is likely that they will receive résumés through email, regular mail, and personal delivery. In addition to determining the methods of receiving résumés, the committee will also set a deadline before they will begin to review résumés. Once the deadline passes, digital or hard copies of each résumé will need to be shared with each committee member to review.

The committee will need to develop a system to review résumés. If they have conducted a national search, it will be impossible to carefully examine hundreds of résumés. Therefore, they will need to agree upon a method to reduce the number of résumés to a manageable number. Depending on the number of applicants, they may need to go through the stack multiple times to reach their target number.

After reviewing résumés, the committee will contact their top candidates and begin to get acquainted. They may ask them to complete a written questionnaire to learn more about their testimony, beliefs, and leadership style. They may begin listening to sample sermons from their top candidates during this time. As they continue to whittle down the list of candidates, they will begin to check references and conduct criminal and credit background checks.

Upon the successful completion of the background checks, the committee will finally begin interviewing candidates. These interviews may be conducted by phone, by video conference, or in person. It's likely they will conduct multiple interviews with one or more candidates.

When the committee finally senses that one individual has risen to the top, they will arrange for the candidate and his family to tour the church property and community. If the church owns a parsonage, they would tour that as well. This visit to the church will probably include a final round of interviews in which a pay package would be presented to the candidate. A formal invitation to be presented to the church would likely soon follow.

As you can see, there are a lot of steps in the Search Phase. The process described above assumes there are no bumps in the road. However, the reality is that the committee might have to stop and back up one or more times during the Search Phase. They might narrow the search down to one candidate who subsequently withdraws his name from consideration. The background check might uncover a red flag. Assuming all goes according to plan, the Search Phase will probably last at least six months. If any unforeseen challenges arise, this phase could take twelve months or more. So again, be patient!

During this phase, updates from the committee might be few and far between until they are ready to present a candidate. I hope that now you understand the reasons for their silence. While the steps taken in the Setup and Study Phases are somewhat predictable, the Search Phase is when the road often becomes crooked and is filled with bumps and potholes!

Your Role in the Search

- **Review:** The Search Phase is usually the longest and most unpredictable phase of the Pastor Search Process.

- **Reflect:** How do you respond when you face significant obstacles to completing an important task?

- **Respond:** Identify church members who have served on a Pastor Search Committee in the past. Ask them about their experience, particularly in regard to the unpredictable nature of the Search Phase.

Day 5

The Select and Support Phases

*Go, for this man is my chosen instrument
to take my name to Gentiles, kings, and
Israelites.*
—Acts 9:15

Who could blame Ananias for being a bit apprehensive when God told him to go and lay hands on Saul of Tarsus (Acts 9:13-14)? It was well known that Saul had been zealously persecuting the saints of God in Jerusalem, going from house to house to drag them off to prison. However, on the road to Damascus, Saul had a life-changing encounter with Jesus. The Lord selected Saul to be his *chosen instrument* to accomplish a specific purpose. That was his calling.

God is still calling men and women to serve Him in specific ways. In fact, God has already selected the man who will serve as your next pastor. Even now, God is working in his life in such a way that he will eventually be overwhelmed by God's call to your church. It is the duty of your Pastor Search Committee to simply discover his identity. In His perfect timing, the Lord will reveal that man to your committee, and they will soon reveal him to you and your fellow church members. That's what happens during the **Select Phase**.

Once the Search Committee feels confident that they have found the man God is calling to be your next pastor, they will contact the remaining candidates to inform them. Then they will schedule a weekend when the prospective pastor and his family will be introduced to the congregation. The weekend will probably consist of different times when individual groups can meet and talk with the prospective pastor. He might first meet with the deacons. Later, he might meet with the Sunday school teachers, the youth group, or the senior adults. The Search Committee will confirm all those details with the candidate.

Then, usually at least one week prior to the scheduled Sunday, the committee will make the announcement to the church and share the schedule of opportunities to meet the prospective pastor. They might also share a biographical profile of the candidate and his family. In this age of social media, the committee might ask you to refrain from publicly disclosing any identifiable information online about the candidate in order to protect his current ministry.

After the prospective pastor has completed the weekend's activities, the congregation will follow the procedures described in your church's Constitution and Bylaws in order to vote on the motion to extend a call to the candidate. After the vote, the Search Committee chairperson should immediately contact the candidate to share the results of the vote. If the vote is affirmative, the chairperson will ask for verbal acceptance, understanding that the candidate may need a few days for prayer before accepting. Once the candidate has accepted the call, the Search Committee will announce the outcome at the next worship service.

While the first three phases could potentially take several months each, the Select Phase should not take long, assuming that the vote is affirmative. While many church members falsely believe that the Pastor Search Process begins with the Search Phase and ends with the Select Phase, the final phase should continue long after your new pastor begins his ministry at your church.

As your new pastor begins to transition to your church, there will be many opportunities to support him and his family. This is known as the **Support Phase**.

First, the church should assist in the moving process. If possible, the church should cover any applicable moving expenses. In addition, the church should provide meals for the pastor's family during the actual move. If he has children, why not volunteer to provide childcare so he and his wife can concentrate on getting settled into their new home?

After the move, the Search Committee or other church leaders should conduct an orientation for the new pastor. If not discussed during the interview process, information should be shared about the way the church operates. Possible topics include business meetings, business reimbursements, days off, church practices regarding the ordinances, etc. In addition, someone from the church should be responsible for introducing the new pastor to community leaders and other local pastors, as well as appropriate denominational leaders.

Another way to support your new pastor will be to help him and his family get adjusted to their new community (if applicable). Perhaps you can help enroll their children in the local school, provide information about service providers in the community, or help with potential employment opportunities for the pastor's wife. There are dozens of ways you can help them adjust.

Finally, the church can go the extra mile to provide ongoing support for your new pastor and his family. Perhaps you can develop a Pastor's Prayer Team that meets with the pastor simply to provide ongoing prayer support for his ministry. Perhaps a Celebrations Team can help the church celebrate the pastor's anniversaries, birthdays, and other significant milestones in the life of his family. Who says the Support Phase has to end? One of the best ways to show your pastor and his family that you love and appreciate them is to provide ongoing support throughout his ministry.

Your Role in the Search

- **Review:** After selecting your new pastor, the church should take intentional steps to support him and his family throughout his ministry.

- **Reflect:** After reviewing the five phases, how has your understanding of the search process changed?

- **Respond:** Begin today by making a list of different ways that you and your fellow church members can provide ongoing support for your next pastor.

Week 6 - Be Productive

Even when the office of pastor is vacant, the church is still the church. Unfortunately, church members are often tempted to slack off in their church commitments during an interim period. Church attendance sometimes wanes. However, every member is part of the body of Christ and has a role to fill. If they fail to do so, the whole body suffers (1 Corinthians 12). Therefore, this final week will encourage you to commit to being "all in" during the time when your church may need you the most.

Day 1

The Church Is Still the Church

For just as the body is one and has many parts, and all the parts of that body, though many, are one body – so also is Christ.
—1 Corinthians 12:12

If you were to get to know me, you would quickly learn that I'm a productivity enthusiast. My wife would call me a productivity nerd, but I digress. The bottom line is I like to get things done. To help me do so, I have read several books on the subject. My electronic devices each have dozens of productivity apps, including calendars, to-do lists, project management collaboration, time management tracking, journals, and digital note-taking, just to name a few. If that wasn't enough, I also use a handwritten daily planner to make sure I'm maximizing my time and energy. So, yeah, I guess I am a productivity nerd!

One of the most important lessons I've learned in

my quest to be more productive is that true productivity is not about getting *more* things done, but it is about getting the *right* things done. Right now, although you may be in a season without a pastor, your church still has been given a mission from the God of the universe. There are still things He wants you to do during this interim period. He wants you to be productive.

The apostle Paul wrote his first letter to the Corinthian church to address a multitude of problems within that congregation, including division, sexual immorality, idolatry, and abuse of the Lord's Supper. All were prevalent in that church, and Paul spent the first eleven chapters of his letter correcting those problems. But in the twelfth chapter, he turned his attention to the problem of spiritual gifts.

Perhaps you're wondering, *What's wrong with spiritual gifts? Aren't they good things?* The answer is that the spiritual gifts themselves were not the problem. The issue was that a few members had abused the purpose of the gifts. They had elevated some of the gifts above the others. By doing so, some church members were treated as second-class Christians because they had not received one of the so-called "super" spiritual gifts.

However, Paul quickly and decisively corrected this faulty line of thinking. In 1 Corinthians 12, this seasoned minister addressed two different mindsets that some people had. On one hand, some members felt that the church didn't need them to accomplish its mission. On the other hand, some members felt that they didn't need other church members. Paul's response to both mindsets was that although the church is one body, it is made up of many members, and every part of the body is necessary in order to accomplish the mission.

Some church members mistakenly think that pastors possess "super" spiritual gifts. While James 3:1 indicates that they will be held to a higher standard, that does not mean that pastors are any more important than anyone else in the church. Pastors fulfill a particular role in the body, but there are many other roles to fill as well. Every part of the body is important. Every part of the body is vital. Every part is needed to accomplish God's plan and design for your church – and you are a part of that body.

However, when churches don't have a pastor, church members tend to slack off in their commitments. Attendance can become more sporadic. Service in the church can decrease. Many church members adopt the mindset, "Let's just try to maintain what we're doing and wait on our new pastor before we get busy serving again."

While this mindset is understandable, it is the exact opposite of the approach you actually need to take. Whenever you lose a pastor, you are losing an important part of the body, and the body suffers for it. However, instead of slacking off, other parts of the body need to step up and fill the void that the pastor left until a new pastor is called.

Why? Because the Great Commission still applies whether you have a pastor or not. Lost people in your community are still dying and going to hell every day, even if you don't have a pastor. Church members still need to be discipled, even if you don't have a pastor.

Shut-ins still need to be encouraged, even if you don't have a pastor. Sermons still need to be preached and Bible studies still need to be taught, even if you don't have a pastor.

The church is still the church, even if you don't have a pastor.

Therefore, fight the temptation to slack off during this interim period. Now more than ever, make the commitment to be productive in fulfilling your role in your church during the search.

Your Role in the Search

- **Review:** Your church needs you to be productive now more than ever.

- **Reflect:** When you think of your relationship to your fellow church members, would you be more likely to say, "They don't need me," or "I don't need them"?

- **Respond:** Spend time praying today that God will give you a renewed desire and commitment to serve Him.

Day 2

Fruit Inspection

But the fruit of the Spirit is love, joy, peace, patience, kindness, goodness, faithfulness, gentleness, and self-control. The law is not against such things.
—Galatians 5:22-23

During the past few years, I've made several adjustments to my eating habits, and I eat much more fruit now than I did in my younger days. However, I'm quite picky about the fruit I eat. Whenever I go to the grocery store, I take time to inspect my options before selecting the pieces of fruit I will purchase. As I examine the bananas, I want to make sure they are ripe enough to eat within the next couple of days, but I also want to make sure they are not so ripe that they will turn brown within the next couple of days.

I'm even more selective with my apples. While I like several varieties, Golden Delicious are my favorite. I usually don't buy a prepackaged bag, though, because I want to inspect each apple for myself. I want to make sure there are no soft spots or bruises. Because I use a slicer that cuts the entire apple at the same time, I also look for apples without a curved core. I pick up each apple and inspect it before placing it in my basket. I only want the best!

As you make the commitment to be productive during this season without a pastor, the Bible teaches that God wants us to bear fruit. In John 15:8, Jesus says, *My Father is glorified by this: that you produce much fruit and prove to be my disciples.* Therefore, the question that needs to be answered is, What type of fruit does God expect you and me to produce?

A popular answer to this question is regarding your level of service in the church. Indeed, much of our focus this week will be on encouraging you to begin to serve or to continue serving while you wait on your next pastor. However, serving is not the only type of fruit God wants us to produce. In fact, it's not even the most important.

As you read Paul's list of the fruit of the Spirit above, notice that most of the fruit are not external activities that you do, but internal attitudes about who you are. Here is another way to say this: *Who you are in Christ is more important than what you do for Christ.*

In the days ahead, we will discuss that what you do for the Lord matters – a lot. However, if we serve the Lord without the proper internal motives and spiritual fruit, our service is nullified. In 1 Corinthians 13:1-3, Paul makes this point clearly: *If I speak human or* angelic tongues, but do not have love, I am a noisy gong or a clanging cymbal. If I have the gift of prophecy and understand all mysteries and all knowledge, and if I have all faith so that I can move mountains but do not have love, I am nothing. And if I give away all my possessions, and if I give over my body in order to boast but do not have love, I gain nothing.* Paul teaches that spiritual activity is of little value if it's not accompanied by the proper spiritual motivations.

Jesus makes the same point in Matthew 7:21-23: *Not everyone who says to me, "Lord, Lord," will enter the kingdom of heaven, but only the one who does the will of my Father in heaven. On that day many will say to me, "Lord, Lord, didn't we prophesy in your name, drive out demons in your name, and do many mighty miracles in your name?" Then I will announce to them, "I never knew you. Depart from me, you lawbreakers!"* In other words, performing many mighty spiritual works apart from a proper spiritual relationship with the Lord accomplishes nothing of eternal value.

Let me say it again: *Who you are in Christ is more important than what you do for Christ.* Therefore, if you want to be productive for the Lord during this interim period, you must first take the time to inspect your internal spiritual fruit. Are you loving? Are you joyful? Are you a person of peace, or do you stir up division and conflict? Are you patient? Are you kind? Would others describe you as someone who maintains self-control?

Take time to inspect your spiritual fruit. Pray and ask the Lord to help you identify the type of fruit you are producing. If He reveals that you are producing the proper fruit, praise the Lord! If He reveals that your spiritual fruit doesn't pass the inspection, confess that to Him and ask Him to help you begin to bear much fruit in the days ahead to the glory of His name. Tomorrow, we'll discuss more about how you can do so.

Your Role in the Search

- **Review:** Who you are in Christ is more important than what you do for Christ.

- **Reflect:** When you think about bearing fruit for the Lord, what types of fruit usually come to your mind?

- **Respond:** Pray and ask the Lord to help you identify the type of fruit you are producing. If adjustments are needed, confess that to the Lord and ask Him to help you bear the proper fruit – beginning today.

Day 3

Abide in Christ

Abide in me, and I in you. As the branch cannot bear fruit by itself, unless it abides in the vine, neither can you, unless you abide in me. I am the vine; you are the branches. Whoever abides in me and I in him, he it is that bears much fruit, for apart from me you can do nothing.
—John 15:4-5 (ESV)

Our family recently welcomed a new puppy into our home. We've had other dogs before, but this is our first puppy. His name is Shadow, and he does what puppies do. He chews on things, he has accidents in the house, he wakes us up earlier than we'd prefer – and he has brought so much enjoyment to our family. As a puppy, Shadow has to be trained to stop those bad behaviors and to start good ones. So far, he has learned to sit, he has learned to bark on command, and he has learned to abide.

Wait, what?

As we're rapidly approaching the end of this book, I wanted to make sure you were still paying attention. I don't know about you, but the word *abide* is not included as a regular part of my vocabulary. So I don't actually use the term *abide* with our puppy, but I did teach him to "stay." That's what abide means. It means to remain or stay.

If you want to be productive during this season without a pastor, Jesus lists a prerequisite in the Scripture passage above: you must abide in Him. You must stay close to Him. You must remain in a personal relationship with Him. It is impossible to produce any lasting spiritual fruit without abiding in Jesus Christ.

So how can you abide in Christ as a member of the church during the search? Here are several ways:

Continue to trust the Lord. As a reminder, there are going to be times when the search process doesn't go as planned or doesn't go the way you'd prefer. Maybe things don't happen as quickly as you'd like. Abiding in Christ means that you continue to trust in the Lord in those moments. If you will trust that He is in control, you won't feel compelled to take matters into your own hands.

Continue in daily Bible study. In order to stay in a close relationship with the Lord, you must spend time with Him in His Word. In fact, Jesus says that this is one of the signature signs of a true disciple: *If you abide in my word, you are truly my disciples, and you will know the truth, and the truth will set you free* (John 8:31-32 ESV). However, multiple studies show that many church members don't read the Bible on a daily basis. This book has provided opportunities for you to read the Word daily, but there is no reason for you to stop once you complete this study. Abide in His Word.

Continue in daily prayer. The best relationships are always two-sided. While Bible study provides the opportunity for God to speak to you, prayer gives you the chance to speak to God. What an incredible privilege to talk to the God of the universe and to know that He listens to us through Jesus Christ, our mediator (1 Timothy 2:5)! Abide in Him by spending time talking with Him on a daily basis.

Continue to obey Him. One of the easiest ways to determine if you are abiding in Christ is the test of obedience. John writes, *This is how we know that we know him: if we keep his commands. The one who says, "I have come to know him," and yet doesn't keep his commands, is a liar, and the truth is not in him. But whoever keeps his word, truly in him the love of God is made complete* (1 John 2:3-5). Ask yourself, "How well am I obeying the Lord?"

Continue to gather with your church family. As mentioned earlier, church attendance often takes a dip during an interim period. However, remaining faithful to Christ also means remaining faithful to His bride. Don't neglect your church family during this season. Abide in Christ and attend each service of your church unless you are providentially hindered.

Continue to serve the Lord. I alluded to this point during yesterday's reading, and it will be the primary topic of discussion tomorrow. Abiding in Christ also means that you continue to serve Him.

If you will commit to abiding in Christ in these ways, you will bear much fruit during this interim period.

Your Role in the Search

- **Review:** You can only bear spiritual fruit if you abide in Christ.

- **Reflect:** In what ways are you abiding in Christ? Are there any ways that you have room for improvement?

- **Respond:** Spend time praying today that God will give you a renewed desire and commitment to serve Him.

Day 4

Gifted to Serve

Now there are different gifts, but the same
Spirit. There are different ministries, but the
same Lord. And there are different activi-
ties, but the same God produces each gift in
each person. A manifestation of the Spirit is
given to each person for the common good.
—1 Corinthians 12:4-7

Every kid has a favorite gift, and I can still remember mine. As a child of the 1980s, I collected several Teenage Mutant Ninja Turtles action figures. However, there was one figure in particular that I wanted more than any other. His name was Triceraton. I begged my mother for him for months, but she refused. I tried to bargain with her, but still no Triceraton. I was so desperate that I even offered to give up McDonald's Happy Meals, but still nothing.

But as I tore open the neatly wrapped packages

on Christmas morning, I came face-to-face with the greatest gift I would ever receive as a child. Big and orange and decked out in his shiny armor, Triceraton was ready for battle. I couldn't have been happier, and neither could my parents.

As a parent myself, I love to give gifts to my children. One question we ask our kids after every Christmas is simply, "What was your favorite gift?" This past year, our youngest son's favorite gift was a remote-controlled car, while our oldest son's favorite was a Star Wars Lego set.

As our heavenly Father, God also delights in giving good gifts to His children (Matthew 7:11). If you are a born-again Christian, He has given you a spiritual gift. This is true for every member of your church, as 1 Corinthians 12:4-7 makes clear.

Peter explains why God gave us each a gift: *Just as each one has received a gift, use it to serve others, as good stewards of the varied grace of God* (1 Peter 4:10). In other words, God has graciously given you a spiritual gift for a purpose. He wants you to use it to serve Him, with or without a pastor.

Therefore, if you want to utilize your spiritual gift, you must first know what it is. There are several good tools you can use to assist you in this discovery process. A simple online search for "spiritual gift inventory" will yield a multitude of options. You might also want to check with your church leaders, for there may already be a tool your church has designated for this purpose.

While these assessments are helpful, I would recommend using them alongside a study of the biblical passages on the topic. In addition to 1 Corinthians 12, you can also find the Bible's teachings on spiritual gifts in Romans 12:3-8, Ephesians 4:11-12, and 1 Peter 4:10-11. As you read these passages, prayerfully ask, "What am I good at? In what ways do I enjoy serving? What am I passionate about?" As you study Scripture, use good tools, and ask yourself questions like these, the Lord will show you how He has gifted you.

After you've discovered your spiritual gifts, the only thing left is to get busy utilizing them! If you're already plugged in and serving in your church, keep it up. If you discover that you are serving in ways that you're not gifted, that's fine. While I don't recommend abruptly quitting without someone else assuming your responsibilities, you should make a transition plan as soon as it is feasible so you can begin to serve in the ways that God has gifted you. Who knows? By doing so, you may also open up the opportunity for someone else in your church to begin serving in the ways God has gifted them.

If you are not currently serving in your church, remember that God has given you a gift for a reason. He wants you to use it. As Peter explained, using your gift is a way of being a good steward of God's grace. Therefore, look for ways to begin using your gift today. If you are gifted to teach, look for opportunities to teach. If you are gifted in hospitality, look for ways to be hospitable. If you are gifted with a love for children, begin changing diapers for the glory of God. If you still have trouble finding a place to serve, talk to others in your church who can help you get plugged in.

As a parent, few things bring me greater pleasure

than to see my kids enjoying the gifts I give them. I imagine that as we joyfully serve the Lord with the gifts He has given us, our heavenly Father is pleased as well.

Your Role in the Search

- **Review:** God has given us spiritual gifts in order to serve Him in the context of our local church.

- **Reflect:** Do you know your spiritual gift(s)? If so, are you using them to serve in your church?

- **Respond:** Read the four Scripture passages listed above on the topic of spiritual gifts. Spend time in prayer today thanking the Lord for His grace in giving you such a precious gift.

Day 5

The Mission Continues

Jesus came near and said to them, "All authority has been given to me in heaven and on earth. Go, therefore, and make disciples of all nations, baptizing them in the name of the Father and of the Son and of the Holy Spirit, teaching them to observe everything I have commanded you. And remember, I am with you always, to the end of the age."
—Matthew 28:18-20

'm a fan of good movies. In the late 1990s, I watched a phenomenal war film starring Tom Hanks called *Saving Private Ryan*. It is set during the invasion of Normandy in World War II, and it tells the story of four brothers who went off to war, with three of them being killed in action. There's an emotional scene when their mother learns the news of her sons' deaths at the same time. The movie then shifts to a small group of soldiers who are given the mission to locate the surviving brother and send him home to his grieving mother. Eight men are sent to save one.

As this small band of servicemen try to locate Private Ryan, they have several encounters with the enemy. By the end of the movie, the group finds Private Ryan, but not before the majority of the soldiers have given their own lives in the process. It's an unforgettable epic of sacrifice and heroism as these men are willing to do whatever it takes to accomplish their mission of saving Private Ryan. This message is certainly inspiring for the church as we seek to accomplish our far greater mission.

If you've been a church member for long, you're probably familiar with the Scripture passage above, known as the Great Commission. Jesus issued it to His disciples right after His resurrection, and it has been the mission of the church for the past two thousand years. As you consider how you and your church can accomplish this mission during this interim season, consider some characteristics of the Great Commission.

First, there's the *priority* of the Great Commission. As Jesus begins, He tells His disciples that all authority in heaven and on earth has been given to Him. That means there's nothing in all of creation that is outside the authority of Jesus, including you and me. When Jesus begins a sentence like that, He means business, so we should pay attention and obey whatever He says. Therefore, the Great Commission must be one of the highest priorities of your life and of your church's ministry efforts. This doesn't change, even when you don't have a pastor.

Second, there's the *purpose* of the Great Commission. After Jesus reminds the disciples of His authority, He tells them the goal: Make disciples of Jesus among all nations. Lead as many as possible to a saving faith in Jesus Christ. Rescue men, women, boys, and girls from every people, tribe, tongue, and nation from a sentence of eternal judgment. That's it. That's the purpose of the Great Commission. The reality is that countless numbers of people die every day apart from Christ and enter into this hopeless eternity. The world doesn't care if your church doesn't have a pastor. They still need Jesus.

Third, there's the *process* of the Great Commission. It's a simple process: the church is to go, baptize, and teach. We go across the street and around the world to tell people about Jesus. Whenever someone expresses a desire to follow Jesus, we baptize them *in the name of the Father and of the Son and of the Holy Spirit.* Then we teach them to obey all that the Lord has commanded us. While your pastor will play a part in these activities, they are not reserved solely for your pastor. You can do these things right now!

Finally, there's the *promise* of the Great Commission. Jesus concludes by reassuring the disciples that He will be with them *always, to the end of the age.* This is huge, so don't miss it! Jesus promises that He will always be with us. He tells us, *You will receive power when the*

*Holy Spirit has come on you, and you will be my wit-
nesses in Jerusalem, in all Judea and Samaria, and to
the end of the earth* (Acts 1:8). Jesus has empowered us
with the Holy Spirit to fulfill the mission.

Therefore, even though you don't have a pastor, you're
not alone! You have been given the same Spirit that
empowered Peter to preach on the day of Pentecost
when three thousand people got saved (Acts 2:14-41).
You have been given the same Spirit that led Philip to
the Ethiopian eunuch so he could share the gospel with
him (Acts 8:26-40). You have been given the same Spirit
that empowered the disciples to boldly proclaim the
gospel to the point that they were described as turning
the world upside down (Acts 17:6). If you are a child of
God, that same Spirit lives in you, and He will never
leave you nor forsake you!

You might not have a pastor right now, but you do
have the Holy Spirit. Therefore, you have everything
you need to carry out the mission during this interim
season. When your next pastor arrives, he can join in
the good work that you and your church are already
doing to reach as many people as possible for Jesus, both
locally and globally. So what are you waiting for? With
the power of the Holy Spirit, go engage in the mission!

Your Role in the Search

- **Review:** Your church has been empowered by the Spirit to engage in the Great Commission, even while you are without a pastor.

- **Reflect:** Have you ever led someone to faith in Christ? If so, describe how it made you feel.

- **Respond:** Make a list of people in your life who have not made professions of faith. Begin to pray for them on a daily basis, and look for opportunities to share the gospel.

Appendix

Small-Group Leader Guide

This guide provides suggestions for leading a small-group study of the contents of this book. The suggestions that follow are designed to help you facilitate an introductory session and six group sessions. Group sessions are designed to be fifty minutes to one hour in length, and they call for a high degree of member participation and discussion. Your primary job will be to serve as a guide and facilitator.

Please note that, depending on the circumstances surrounding your previous pastor's departure, emotions may be running high among group members. Members may indeed be sad, mad, glad, or indifferent, and they may have difficulty understanding why other group members do not feel the same way. Take special care to promote charity among your group members so your church can maintain unity as you navigate this season of transition together.

For accompanying small group resources, including videos, additional discussion questions, and other resources, visit **churchsearchbook.com/smallgroups**.

Supplies for Each Session

- Extra copies of *The Church During the Search*
- Extra Bibles
- Attendance sheet
- Pens or pencils for each participant
- Snacks and refreshments (encourage everyone to bring something)

General Outline for Each Session

While you may revise the order to better accommodate your context, each session should include the following elements:

- Greet each participant as they arrive.
- Begin each session in prayer. After you cover the contents of Week 4, spend time during the final two sessions praying for your church, the Pastor Search Committee, your next pastor, and your next pastor's family.
- Read the primary Bible verses for the session.

- Play the session's optional teaching video available from churchsearchbook.com/smallgroups.

- Lead the group in a conversation, using the session's discussion questions as a guide.

- Provide a brief overview of the daily readings to be completed prior to the next group session.

- Close in prayer.

Introductory Session

Text: Ecclesiastes 3:1-14

Discussion Questions:

1. Have you ever been a member of a church during a pastor search? If so, share about your experience.

2. What hopes do you have as your church begins the search for a new pastor? What fears?

3. How does Ecclesiastes 3:1-14 comfort you as you enter this season without a pastor?

4. What role does the average church member have in the church during the search? What activities should they be involved in?

5. What do you hope to learn from this study?

Reading Assignment: Introduce Week 1: Be Prepared. Encourage participants to read the Introduction and Days 1-5 prior to the next group session.

Session 1

Text: Deuteronomy 31:1-23

Discussion Questions:

1. What stood out to you from the readings this week?

2. What lessons did you discover about the transition of leadership from Moses to Joshua in Deuteronomy 31:1-23?

3. Once a decision is made about calling an interim pastor, how will you continue to support your church, especially if you disagree with the decision?

4. What are some practical ways you can avoid second-guessing the Pastor Search Committee when there is no news?

5. How do you normally respond when your plans are changed?

6. Why is it helpful to distinguish the pastor's salary from the total compensation package?

Reading Assignment: Introduce Week 2: Be Informed. Encourage participants to read the five corresponding daily readings prior to the next group session.

Session 2

Text: Psalm 23

Discussion Questions:

1. What stood out to you from the readings this week?

2. Did any of the four primary roles of a shepherd discussed from Psalm 23 surprise you?

3. How do you respond when you hear a sermon from a difficult passage?

4. How do Christians typically respond when confronted with a false teaching or a personal sin? How do you respond?

5. Given the fact that Jesus could only be at one place at one time during His earthly ministry, how should that change your church's expectations about your next pastor?

6. Why do you think the pastoral qualifications listed in 1 Timothy 3:1-7 focus more on the internals rather than the externals?

Reading Assignment: Introduce Week 3: Be Humble. Encourage participants to read the five corresponding daily readings prior to the next group session.

Session 3

Text: Philippians 2:1-8

Discussion Questions:

1. What stood out to you from the readings this week?

2. Why is it difficult for a church to have unity without humility?

3. What are some examples of unrealistic expectations for pastors? How can those expectations be adjusted?

4. Have you identified any potential land mines in your church that need to be disarmed before you call your next pastor?

5. How can your church honor the past, but look to the future?

6. Have you allowed any of your desires for your next pastor to become demands?

Reading Assignment: Introduce Week 4: Be Prayerful. Encourage participants to read the five corresponding daily readings prior to the next group session.

Session 4

Text: Luke 6:12-16

Discussion Questions:

1. What stood out to you from the readings this week?

2. How did you feel after reading in Luke 6:12-16 that Jesus prayed all night long before selecting His apostles?

3. Prior to this week's readings, had prayer been a priority for you during this interim period?

4. Has your perspective toward prayer's role during the search changed after this week's readings? If so, how?

5. Were there any prayer suggestions in this week's readings that were surprising to you?

6. What are some ways your church can encourage regular prayer for your church, your Pastor Search Committee, your next pastor, and your next pastor's family during the search?

Reading Assignment: Introduce Week 5: Be Patient. Encourage participants to read the five corresponding daily readings prior to the next group session.

Session 5

Text: James 5:7-11

Discussion Questions:

1. What stood out to you from the readings this week?

2. We've read several times throughout the book that the average pastor search takes from twelve to eighteen months. How does that make you feel?

3. What does James 5:7-11 teach us about being patient during the search process?

4. Prior to this week's readings, were you aware of the five phases of the search process? If not, which phases were new to you?

5. Why do you think it would be unwise to skip the Setup and Study Phases and jump right into the Search Phase?

6. What are some practical steps you and your fellow members can take to ensure that your church does not forget the Support Phase?

Reading Assignment: Introduce Week 6: Be Productive. Encourage participants to read the five corresponding daily readings prior to the final group session.

Session 6

Text: 1 Corinthians 12:4-27

Discussion Questions:

1. What stood out to you from the readings this week?

2. Why is it important to think of the church as a body, with Christ as the head?

3. Why do you think there is a tendency for church members to become unproductive during an interim period?

4. Do you agree with the statement, "Who you are in Christ is more important than what you do for Christ"? Why or why not?

5. Do you know your spiritual gifts? If so, how are you using them to serve the Lord?

6. How can you and your fellow church members continue to fulfill the Great Commission while the church continues the search for a new pastor?

Reading Assignment: Encourage participants to review the contents of this book throughout the search.

About the Author

Jason Lowe serves as the Associational Mission Strategist for the Pike Association of Southern Baptists. In this role, he has helped numerous churches navigate the transition from one pastor to the next. In addition, he serves as the Executive Pastor of First Baptist Church in Pikeville, Kentucky. Jason and his wife, Brandi, have two sons: Isaiah and Noah. You can connect with him at jasonalowe.com.

Congregational Covenant

To be used by the congregation at the conclusion of studying The Church During the Search. *It can be read responsively during the worship service or signed privately.*

As a member of our church during the search:

- I will strive to prepare myself to expect the unexpected during the pastor search process. I will make every effort to worship the Lord, even when I don't know who will be preaching on Sunday. I will strive to serve in the church when things don't go as planned or when I don't hear any updates. I will prepare myself for the ups and downs of the pastor search process, trusting that God is working out His plan for our church in His timing.

- I will strive to be better informed about the biblical roles of a pastor to feed, lead, protect, and comfort his flock during the pastor search process. I will seek to become well acquainted with the biblical qualifications for a pastor, and I will seek to take opportunities to encourage those entrusted with the responsibility to identify our next pastor. I look forward to supporting my next pastor as he faithfully strives to fulfill the biblical roles as my spiritual shepherd.

- I will strive to be humble during the pastor search process, working diligently to place the needs and interests of other church members above my own. I will strive to avoid allowing my desires to become demands, either of the Pastor Search Committee or of my next pastor and his family. I will seek to disarm any land mines before my next pastor arrives. I will honor the past, but I will also make every effort to look to the future and support the current and future ministry endeavors of my church.

- I will strive to be prayerful during the pastor search process. I will strive to pray that my church will make these six commitments during the search. I will strive to pray for the Pastor Search Committee as they faithfully and sacrificially go about their work. I will make every effort to pray for my next pastor to sense God's leading to our church. I will strive to pray that his family will be able to make a smooth transition to our church as well.

- I will strive to be patient during the pastor search process. I recognize that while the average pastor search process lasts for 12-18 months, our process could take longer. I will seek to trust in God's timing, and I will make every effort to refrain from placing any additional pressure on the Pastor Search Committee if they fail to present a pastor candidate on my preferred timetable.

- I will strive to be productive during the pastor search process, recognizing that the church is still the church even while we don't have a pastor. I will continue to cultivate a growing relationship with the Lord through my practice of the personal spiritual disciplines. I will seek to use my spiritual gifts to serve the Lord and His church, and I will make every effort to avoid slacking off in any of my current church commitments. I will also faithfully seek to share the gospel as God gives me the opportunity with those outside the church.

Sign and Date

Download a printable Congregational Covenant at

www.jasonalowe.com/other-book-resources